Unlocking

the

of

Facilitation

Published by
Impetus Books
Austin, TX
www.impetus.pw

Special discounts are available on quantity purchases by
schools, corporations, associations, and others. Book is available in both print and E-book formats. For details, contact the
publisher using the above website.

ISBN-10: 0-9897602-3-5
ISBN-13: 978-0-9897602-3-2

Cover photo by Juskteez Vu
Cover design, layout design, and all illustrations
by Sam Killermann

Published January 2016
2 4 6 8 10 9 7 5 3

to the wary and the passionate

Table of Contents

"It's still magic even if you know how it's done."

- Terry Pratchett

Preface

"Thrown over a precipice,
you fall or else you fly."

- Margaret Atwood

n the fall of 2015, we were brought into a small town in rural Washington. It was the type of town where you meet welders—and they introduce themselves to you as welders. We were training facilitators at a local university, and we were also asked to facilitate a town hall meeting for the community at large. The town hall was intended to be an educational session about diverse genders and sexualities, in response to the university's efforts to be more inclusive of folks of all gender identities (and transgender students in particular).

Minutes into the open forum, after we had just barely had the chance to define what is meant by the initialism LGBTQ, a welder sitting in the back of the room raised his hand. He was sitting in the middle of the back wall, with his legs spread wide, leaning back in his chair with his arms firmly crossed. The look on his face was equal parts disinterested and impassioned. We knew he was a welder, because it was one of the first things he said when we called on him. He continued to say something like the following:

"I just don't understand why any of this matters. It shouldn't matter. I'm straight, and I don't ask people to make a big deal of my sexuality. Just mind your own business, and I'll mind mine. Some people these days make big issues out of nothing, putting, like, gay bumper stickers on their car and stuff. It seems like they just want attention. You never see any straight pride parades. I don't have any straight bumper stickers on my truck. Everyone gets it. We get it. I mean, it's starting to feel like it's harder to be a straight, White, man nowadays, than anything else."

Without looking at one another, or exchanging a word, we both had the same series of thoughts, and we know this now because we debriefed the entire town hall.

"When that welder guy first spoke," we said to each other, "did you think:" (1) *Dang, this escalated quickly*; (2) *Did that guy just play* All the Hits[1] *in one rant?*; (3) *Do we engage with*

---

1 Imagine oppression being a classic rock band. They're always turning out new stuff, but nobody goes to the concert to hear it. It's impossible to top the hits. And this guy played them all: the "colorblind" approach to oppression ("I don't see difference"), the "it's not a big deal" (to a person with the dominant group identities), the "straight pride parade" argument (a reprisal of the "White history month" Billboard Hit), and the forever-chart-topper "reverse discrimination" jam session.

*this comment, knowing that doing so will likely redefine the en-
tire town hall, and anything we planned to cover is susceptible to
being devoured by the discussion that would follow?*; and (4) *If
we engaged, where do we even start?*

We chose to engage, and the next hour flew by. A clear
dichotomy presented itself in the room: those onboard with
inclusion of marginalized genders and sexualities, and those
opposed. These factions represented their views loudly, and
we did everything we could to keep the conversation productive, civil, and more "Town Hall" than "Wild West Saloon
Brawl."

We used every trick we had up our sleeve.

We engaged compassionately with the welder and his
comrades throughout the event—hearing their concerns,
their realities, and then providing alternatives that they
could consider. We affirmed the folks who were frustrated
with the lack of inclusion, or lack of "progress" in the town
(The phrase "...in two-thousand and fifteen..." was peppered
into a lot of statements. *"How are we still having this pushback
in two-thousand and fifteen?"*).

At a turning point in the discussion, the welder revealed
to us a time that he stumbled into a gay bar ("One of *their*
bars," as he put it) by accident, and knew immediately he
wasn't welcome.

"I could just feel it," he said. He wasn't welcome there,
and he didn't like that. It didn't feel fair to him. But that's
just how the world is, he implied.

We asked, "What did it feel like when you didn't feel welcome?"

"It sucked."

We let that sink in, then replied, "That's a terrible feeling,
to not feel welcome. And it's that feeling that we—in this

town hall, and in the work that the university is doing—are trying to prevent. There are lots of people who, right now, feel that way in the majority of spaces they enter. Because when you're not the default, to not be explicitly included is to be implicitly excluded."

His entire body language transformed. He leaned forward in his seat, uncrossed his arms and propped himself up with his elbow on his knee, and his face softened. He didn't reply as much as he simply acknowledged. And this change shifted the energy in the room.

Both of us saw it, felt it, and did a telepathic "High-five" when it happened. We know this, because we debriefed it after. Did we telepathically high-five when the welder engaged in the conversation?

After the town hall, the welder came up to us, and did something that, for us, is emblematic of facilitation magic: he apologized-thanked us.

"I'm really sorry that I wasn't getting it. To be honest, there is still a lot I don't get. But I hadn't thought of things the way that I'm thinking of them now, about all *this stuff*. Nobody talked with me that way before. Thanks for that, and for doing what you're doing." And then he shook our hands before heading out back into his life.

The next morning, we had the second day of our facilitator training at the university. A few of the participants were at the town hall and word had spread about what happened. The first question on everyone's mind was, "How did you *do* that at the town hall last night?"

＊＊＊

When we work to train others to be effective facilitators, we never get to everything. And sometimes it feels like the more ground we cover, the more aware the folks we're training are of how little they know. With that realization comes anxiety and doubt, and the irony is not lost on us: in some ways, our trainings make facilitators feel less competent as facilitators.

No matter how long a train-the-trainer visit is, we never have enough time to explain and share all the nuanced choices we make as a facilitators, how we choose when to engage with antagonistic participants, or everything that is going through our minds the entire time (all the decisions we don't make, as well as the ones we do).

We never get to all the magic tricks.

This is an ever-present frustration for us, because we don't take our responsibilities in facilitator training lightly. We see facilitation as a powerful wand, that in well-trained hands can achieve wonderful, healthy, positive outcomes; and that in untrained hands can lead to disaster and pain. In trying to leave a group with all the techniques they need to be more effective facilitators, to not get to something that we *know* will make a difference in their future trainings is discouraging.

Writing this book was about creating that resource that we could hand to folks and say, "Hey, we didn't get to everything, but never fear: we wrote it down for you."

We have found that most facilitators spend a disproportionate amount of their time learning the content material they'll be communicating, instead of how they'll be communicating it. In some ways, that's a good thing: facilitation is a difficult thing to teach, and is often better learned by experience, so folks focus on what they know they *can* learn from reading. But it's not impossible to learn from reading, and in creating this book we are rising to that challenge.

When we aren't given as much time as we prefer for train-the-trainer visits, it's generally because those folks simply can't afford the extra time to spend on facilitation training. We didn't want to create a book that presented the same barriers.

***

In drafting what we wanted to cover in a book about facilitation, we came up with over 40 important, "can't live without these" things-turned-chapters. Our first draft of a manuscript was trending toward a 400+ page book, which formed into four distinct sections: power in group dynamics, key concepts of facilitation, elements of a training, and developing a facilitation style. **This book** is that second section, reworked, distilled, and polished: the 11 key concepts we think you should know.

We're hoping to encourage people to step into the arena, and also provide support for those already seasoned by experience, by providing an easily-digestible, quickly-helpful resource to enhance learning about the technique of facilitation.

And in doing so, we recognize that (like in our train-the-trainer visits) we are leaving out as much as we are putting in. So while this book is self-contained in its learning and mission, we're also going to publish the other three sections—plus the section that became this book; indeed, an attempt at collecting everything we've learned into one book—as *A Guide to Facilitation: The Social Justice Advocate's Handbook*.

We are two passionate social justice educators who believe in the power of facilitation. We've spent close to two decades trying to sort through this style of engagement, and we want to share what we've learned so far with you.

Introduction

"Every great magic trick consists of three parts or acts. The first part is called the *Pledge*. The magician shows you something ordinary: a deck of cards, a bird or a man.... The second act is called the *Turn*. The magician takes the ordinary something and makes it do something extraordinary. Now you're looking for the secret, but you won't find it, because of course you're not really looking. You don't really want to know. You want to be fooled. But you wouldn't clap yet. Because making something disappear isn't enough; you have to bring it back. That's why every magic trick has a third act, the hardest part, the part we call the *Prestige*."

- *Cutter, in* The Prestige

Y ou, like us, believe that facilitation is important. That didn't take a mentalist to divine: it's why you're reading this book, and why we're writing it. You've witnessed the magic of facilitation. Maybe it was when you realized you were signing up for classes based on the teacher, instead of the subject. Or after a day-long training where you found yourself saying something like, "I feel like we've only been together for an hour, and at the same time like we've learned enough to fill two weeks."

Or maybe you've noticed the absence of magic. Going to a workshop you knew you were going to love, and leaving unsure of how someone made you feel so ambivalent about your own passion.

If you've had experience in front of a group, you know some of what goes on behind the curtain. If you haven't, you can still draw on what you know from being in the crowd. You've seen the effects of facilitation, and in this book we reveal the secrets behind our favorite tricks. Before we get to that, let's make sure we're on the same page when talking about "facilitation."

WHAT IS FACILITATION?

In this book, we use "facilitation" to describe a style of engaging others toward a goal. We generally assume that goal is learning, which we use in the broadest of ways: learning content knowledge, learning about oneself and others, or unlearning (our favorite type of learning).

In facilitation, there are two key roles: the facilitator (or facilitators) and the participants. The facilitator is the person responsible for guiding the learning process. We often describe this as being "in the front of the group." The participants are the folks who are expected to be doing the learning.

It can be helpful to think of the facilitator as the captain of a ship. And you can think of the participants as the crew. Now, the members of the crew, together, have what they need to work the ship without the captain. They should know how to hoist the sails, and turn the rudder. Perhaps some of them are newer to this, but the older crew members could fill them in. Without a crew, a captain is unable to maneuver a ship. But a crew would be lost without the captain. It's the captain's vision, coordination, and guidance that enable the crew to work seamlessly together toward their common goal. And the goal is to move the ship from one point to another, avoiding any sandbars, tide pools, or icebergs along the way—and leaving no crewmember behind.

WHEN YOU'RE IN THE PRESENCE OF MAGIC

While there are countless ways to be a great facilitator, there are common threads that link all of the magical facilitation we've experienced:

1. Time flies. Almost every time we've ever been participants in a workshop where the facilitators were on their game, we've wondered where the time went and wanted more.

2. Everyone stays engaged. A great facilitator works in a way that keeps everyone present, learning, and in the work. There may be moments where participants check out, or don't show up for the work that day, but great facilitators pull those participants back into the moment like a rabbit from a hat.

3. Everyone grows, even the facilitator. Facilitation is about actively involving participants in their own learning process, and when that's done well, it means there are plenty of opportunities for the facilitator to learn from the participants.

To do the above seems easy when you're the participant, but requires a deft hand as a facilitator. All of the concepts in this book, in one way or another, will help you facilitate experiences where time flies, everyone is engaged, and everyone grows.

WHO IS THIS BOOK FOR?

This book is for people who, in their professional or personal lives, find themselves responsible for engaging a group of people in a process. Over the years, we've found that a lot of folks we would describe as facilitators don't use the moniker for themselves. We wrote this book for facilitators of all stripes, whether they wear the badge "facilitator" or not: outdoor educators, teachers, social workers, social justice advocates, orientation guides, coaches, group counselors, and other people who find themselves regularly, or occasionally, responsible for helping a group get from point A to another point.

This book is for ourselves ten years ago, when we would have benefited one thousand fold from having access to the learning we've collected since then. Similarly, it's for anyone who identifies as a facilitator, and hasn't had the opportunity to have any formal training, learning, or conversations about the craft.

Facilitators are generally passionate about their content area. Occasionally, we let that passion obstruct our view of the fact that we all have a foot in two fields: whatever our content area is, and facilitation. This book is content agnostic and process intensive. It's all about the latter: how do you best engage a group around learning a topic that is dear to your heart (or integral to your job).

WHAT THIS BOOK ISN'T

This book is *not* a substitute for experience, practice, finding your groove, being in the front of the room, or a passion for people. It's a complement for all of those things, and all of the other things required of great facilitation; a catalyst that will augment your learning from those things; and a source of support and mentorship. This book, in and of itself, is not sufficient to make you a great facilitator, but we don't know many great facilitators who haven't mastered the key concepts espoused here (even if they wouldn't use the same language to describe them as we do).

WHAT THIS BOOK IS: THE 11 KEY CONCEPTS

Over the years we have been training trainers (i.e., teaching folks how to facilitate), we have noticed themes that consistently emerged. These themes were irrespective of content area or cultural trends, universal and evergreen. The 11 concepts introduced and described in this book are, to wit, the highlights of the learning of all those train-the-trainer experiences.

The first two chapters reframe how we think about facilitation. Taken together with the next five chapters, you'll have the framework you need in order to make the most out of the latter five. Chapter eight is the turn, and chapters nine through eleven are our prestige. Here's a more detailed tease at what we're going to cover in this book:

1. **Understanding Facilitation as a Nuanced Skill.** Facilitation is...well...both nuanced and a skill: two things we don't give it enough credit for being. In this chapter we'll talk about why facilitation is a skill, who gets to identify as a facilitator, and the need to practice facilitation.

2. **Facilitation vs. Teaching vs. Lecturing.** Facilitation is a different style of engagement from teaching or lecturing. What makes it different? Why is that difference so important? What are things that we are giving up and gaining by choosing to facilitate?

3. **Being Neutral.** This chapter could also be called "Neutrality is non-existent" or "Neutrality: That would be nice, and so would Santa Claus." Being a facilitator is not about being neutral, but instead about being honest and open with your group about your goals together, and recognizing the implicit bias in those goals.

4. **How to Read a Group.** Start by listening. Get to know them before they get in the room as much as possible, and then pay attention to what they are expressing and sharing in order to know where to go next. Groups are writing a lot about what they need; you just need to start reading.

5. **Both/And is Greater than But/Or.** The power of replacing but with "and" is incredible. Find out why in fa-

cilitation it can change how your participants respond and react and how you respond and react to them. Pulling ourselves out of the duality of either/or, the almighty "and" helps us see multiple realities as feasible and present.

6. The "Yes, and..." Rule. One of the foundational rules of improv has become one of our foundational concepts of facilitation. By adding to someone's reality rather than negating it, you can often learn much more about a person's perspective, understanding, and ideas, than any "no" could ever bring you.

7. Asking Good Questions. Good questions are more than just "open-ended" questions. Good facilitators ask good questions; great facilitators know how to do that every time. We cover what makes a good question, what kind of questions are out there to be asked, and what kind is best in what scenario.

8. Safe Spaces for Vulnerability. Facilitating can be challenging; showing up and really being seen while you're facilitating can be even harder. We explore the impact of vulnerability on facilitation, and how courageous compassion is required to make a space where folks can learn from vulnerability.

9. Triggers. Not all experiences within a training are pleasant or wanted, and sometimes they leave our blood boiling and our heart racing. To be an effective facilitator, it's our responsibility to manage our triggers, and we give you a model for doing just that.

10. Learning from Emotions. Emotions happen. As facilitators, we have a choice of whether to invite emotions into our trainings and what to do when they show up. We'll explore how to make the most of those emotional moments, and the types of powerful learning available when you get ready to wrestle with emotions.

11. Role Modeling Continuous Learning (or The Myth of the Expert). We ask a lot of our participants, but perhaps nothing more important than being open to new learning. As a facilitator, we must lean into our own request, own our journeys, and role model the importance of saying, "I don't know."

ON PRONOUNS AND FOOTNOTES

We're huge fans of the gender neutral singular "they," and in this book we will be using it liberally (already have). If this is going to frustrate you on a "grammar nerd" front, we recommend one of two things: (1) look up the origins of singular "they" usages in English—it's only recently that it's become a grammar faux pas; or (2) get over it.

We use footnotes to provide both sources for references mentioned in the text, and frivolous asides or back story from a personal perspective. The general rule can be that if there's a footnote, it's not required reading to make sense of the text that follows, but it's always recommended.

Finally, instead of including a recommended readings, references, or resources appendix in the book, we will have a living version of this on the book's website at the following link: http://facilitationmagic.com/resources.

LET'S BEGIN.

Magicians don't call what they do *tricks*, they call them *effects*. We think that's too perfect, and ith that, let's get into our first chapter, and our first effect: the one that comes after you recognize the nuanced skill that is facilitation.

Understanding Facilitation as a Nuanced Skill

"Art is not what you see, but what you make others see."

- Edgar Degas

Facilitation is a challenging subject to teach. It's in the face of this challenge, we suspect, that most folks don't even bother trying to formally teach it. Most facilitators learn how to facilitate in one of four ways, presented here in most-to-least formal: (1) in a retreat or mini-retreat setting where the material to be facilitated is covered, and a few general pointers about facilitation are presented (e.g., "Ask open-ended questions.... Avoid values statements...."); (2) shadowing or co-facilitating with an experienced facilitator; (3) being a participant in someone else's facilitation and thinking "I could totally do that;" or (4) being given a packet with some instructions, put in front of a room full of people, after someone saying "you can totally do this."

If you've participated in any of the above forms of facilitator training, you may have noticed something we noticed: it's less training on *how* to facilitate, and more training on *what* you'll be facilitating. In this book, and in the following three sections in particular, we are doing the exact opposite. We are presenting to you lessons we've learned—from other facilitators, from unrelated researchers, and from our own 1000+ hours of experience facilitating—focusing on developing the skill that is facilitation.

The primary reason facilitation is so difficult to teach is because of how nuanced it is. There is no one right way to do it (indeed, everyone does it differently); there is no credential or requisite experience necessary (indeed, most of us only have the training mentioned above); and the only way you can get good is by practicing it a lot (indeed, indeed, indeed). In this chapter, we'll expand on these ideas, and in the following chapters, we will dig deep into them.

ELEMENTS OF A NUANCED SKILL

There are a few key things about facilitation that it shares with other nuanced skills (like golf, interior decorating, and pronouncing the word "nuanced"). Understanding these elements—how they affect your ability to facilitate, your perceptions of facilitation or other facilitators—is integral to processing the learning in the following chapters. So what makes a skill nuanced?

EVERYONE DOES IT DIFFERENTLY.

Great facilitators do not all facilitate alike. Some are adept at staying in touch with their participants' moods, energies, and needs; others know just how to keep your attention; others can invite an entire group to participate no matter what the topic. It's easy to be seduced into the idea that there's a "right" way to do it, a model to emulate; but we all have different ways of being great facilitators. There is no one right way.

EVERYONE COMES TO IT FROM DIFFERENT PLACES, WITH DIFFERENT EXPECTATIONS.

Have you ever watched someone golfing and said, "That looks so easy"? Have you ever tried golfing? It's great, if you enjoy a little fresh air to accompany your torture. Some people learn to golf as kids, some take lessons, some have to do it for work, some are naturals, some are not. Facilitation is the same way. There's no one way people come to don the Facilitator Cap, and there is no formal or requisite past experience one needs to do it, nor to do it well. And while it looks easy to some bystanders, facilitation is anything but.

PRACTICE MAKES PERFECT.

We hope this book can expedite your learning process. Our goal here is for you to benefit from a few thousand words of wisdom gleaned from thousands of hours of practice. That said, know that this book is not a substitute for practice in front of a group. Give yourself grace, knowing that regardless of how much you prep, or how fastidiously you apply the lessons from this book, there is going to be a (steep, mountainous, but super fun) learning curve when you get in the front of the room.

RESPECTING (AND APPRECIATING) THE NUANCE OF FACILITATION

Like most great art forms, facilitation, when done well, looks effortless. The facilitator moves and flows and asks and listens, and hours fly by. In a response to powerful facilitation, participants often register comments in feedback forms that allude to "how surprised" they are by how much they learned, or how quickly the time passed. And like most great art forms, there is a masterful intention behind every decision—a vision for the final painting that forms with the first brushstroke.

In the next several chapters, and then in the following two sections of the book, we are going to introduce you to and explain the often-invisible techniques master facilitators use in every training. At first glance, the chapter headings may register as unrelated, or even disinteresting (i.e., *I don't need to know this to facilitate*), but we ask that you trust us: these are the things we wish we had known before starting our facilitator journeys, and we won't lead you astray.

Facilitating vs. Teaching vs. Lecturing

"The greatest sign of success for a teacher is to be able to say, 'The children are now working as if I did not exist.'"

- Maria Montessori

A wise person once said, "If this is a book about facilitation, why is there a chapter about teaching and lecturing?" That person was our first-pass editor (and likely you). It's a fair question. In the last chapter, we talked about the nuance of facilitation, and how facilitation is a tough subject to teach. Well, one of the ways we're hoping to help you understand that nuance is by talking about two things that facilitation isn't—but that it gets confused with, and are as integral to most training or learning experiences as facilitation itself. And besides, what's more nuanced than talking about a thing by talking about what it isn't?

DIFFERENT METHODS WITH THE SAME GOAL: LEARNING

Although we identify as educators whose method of choice is facilitation, we also find ourselves putting on our teacher or lecturer caps. All three methods of achieving learning have their perks, and to know which is best when, we must first understand the differences among lecturing, teaching, and facilitating.

Two helpful things to consider when dissecting the differences among lecturing, teaching, and facilitating are (1) the levels of **agency** the educator and learners hold over the content covered; and (2) the level of **active participation** required by the educator and learners. Let's define these concepts so we're all on the same page:

Agency, in this case, can be thought of as the "capacity of individuals to act independently and to make their own free choices" (Wikipedia) for what content will be learned.

Active participation is the level at which the person is engaging the other people involved—vocally, externally, and in a way that affects the outcome of the overall learning.

More simply, agency is who is deciding what's learned, and participation is how that learning is achieved.

LECTURING: HIGH EDUCATOR AGENCY & PARTICIPATION, LOW LEARNER AGENCY & PARTICIPATION

Lecturing has achieved a negative connotation in most

social circles, but it is not without its value. Lecturing can be thought of as any time the educator is speaking directly to the learners in an uninterrupted way until their point is made. Beyond the bias that the word "lecture" evokes, our main concerns are that lecturing is often overused and sometimes not treated with enough care.

In lecturing, the educator has high agency over the content that will be covered, and also must be actively participating throughout the entire learning experience; whereas the learners have little to no agency, and little to no participation is required. This high level of educator agency and low learner participation is helpful when...

* there is something really specific that needs to be learned, and the group cannot do without it;

* you're crunched for time and have a high level of content to cover;

* the educator holds some specialized knowledge that the group likely does not; and/or

* there is a highly disproportionate ratio of educators-to-learners (there's a reason universities are full of lecture *halls*, not lecture closets).

Lectures are often thought to be long (or really, really, really long if you want to be melodramatic about it), but there is no set length that qualifies a lecture. To emphasize this, we want to introduce you to the idea of mini-lectures (or *lecturettes*, if you wanna gender *everything*), which are short lectures—generally no more than 5-10 minutes—that teach a specific, concrete point.

We use mini-lectures throughout trainings when we want to present a chunk of information before getting feedback or taking questions. We like to thread them through other activities, or material that we also teach and facilitate. If you are hoping to accomplish a training that involves your group, you should avoid lecturing for all (or even most) of the time. Even if the training is incredibly short, back and forth is crucial for participants to feel included and important.

Teaching: Medium Educator Agency & Participation, Medium Learner Agency & Participation

Teaching is the method of learning that we experience the most. It's often confused with lecturing, and is generally the go-to default for achieving a learning goal with a person or a group. While teaching has a lot of value, one of our goals with this book is to get you out of default-mode thinking, and push you to be intentional with all of your choices. Choosing when to (or when not to) teach is an important choice.

Teaching, in the context of a school room, often carries a power dynamic where one person is seen as the "Teacher," meaning the person who holds the knowledge and the ability to disseminate that knowledge, and everyone else is seen as "Students," those without knowledge who need to be taught. This way of thinking is what Paulo Freire calls the "banking model" of education, and while many school teachers (and school systems) ascribe to or perpetuate this form of teaching, it is not the type of teaching we're referring to in this chapter. That understanding of teaching more aligns with what we describe above as lecturing.

In this chapter, we're using "teaching" to describe a co-created relationship between educator and learner. Teaching, as opposed to lecturing, requires that the learner has buy-in, the educator is ever conscious of the learners' wants and needs, and by frequently checking in with the learners, the educator gives the learners opportunities to ask for clarification, redirection, or a deeper understanding of a particular idea.

To put it more simply, one might say that lecturing is done *at* a learner, while teaching is done *with* or *for* a learner.

Teaching is the middle of the road on both the agency and active participation front. In teaching, the educator has medium agency and high active participation; the learner also has medium agency, and medium-to-low active participation. This medium of everything is perfect for learning goals that aren't too hot and aren't too cold. We recommend teaching when...

★ you have a sense of what material needs to be covered, but the group could live without everything, and you're able to head down a few rabbit holes if the group asks;

★ you have a few more minutes available than what it would take to just say all the things, but you don't have buckets of extra time;

★ you know a lot about a particular thing, but you also have a hunch that you're not the only one in the room who does; and/or

★ the group of learners is big, but not so big that you couldn't learn all of their names in a few minutes if you gave it a shot.

Facilitating: Low Educator Agency & Participation, High Learner Agency & Participation

Now that you have a few different ways to think about

lecturing and teaching, you probably already have a strong hunch about what we're going to say about facilitating. And you're probably right: facilitating is everything that lecturing and teaching *isn't*. As we've moved through the three concepts using agency and participation as our anchors, you've likely noticed a trend: lecturing, teaching, and facilitation exist on a continuum of sorts, with lecturing and facilitation being polar opposites, while teaching is in between the two.

In facilitating, the educator has low agency over what content will be learned, and a low level of active participation; whereas the learners have a medium to high amount of agency, and a high amount of active participation is required for it to work. Facilitating is communism for learning: it's decentralized, it requires everyone's involvement, and Sam's uncle will get mad if you bring it up at Thanksgiving dinner.

Don't mistake the low educator agency and participation as a sign that the educator can check out. Facilitation requires an incredible amount of focus, intention, and engagement from the facilitator—even if they aren't doing most of the talking.

Facilitation is often activity-based. Activities prompt a group to participate in a scenario that is an abstract representation of the intended learning; then, through processing that scenario (i.e. talking about the experience), the learning is solidified. However, facilitation can take a variety of forms, including games, discussion, reflection, dialogue, and more.

This whole book is about facilitating, so we're not going to spend too much more time on it in this chapter, but there are a few times in particular we think facilitation is the bee's knees. Facilitating is perfect when...

* you can leave most of the decision-making of the exact things the group will learn to the group itself;

* you have plenty of time;

* there is no doubt that the learners, as a community, already have some or most of the knowledge you're hoping to learn, and might just need some help realizing it, or organizing their way of thinking about what they already know; and/or

* there isn't an overwhelming ratio of learners to educators, or you're able to easily convert some of the learners into educators (e.g., break the big group into smaller groups, and assign each group a facilitator of sorts).

KNOWING WHAT TO USE WHEN: CONSIDER REQUIREMENTS AND RESTRAINTS

There are countless recommendations we could make, beyond the ones we made above, about when it's right to lean on lecturing, teaching, or facilitating; but most of them would come down to our subjective bias (don't think we have to spell out what ours would be, considering the title and subtitle of this book). Instead, we recommend you consider the requirements and restraints of any learning situation, and then pick the method of engagement best for the moment.

In this case, the **requirements** are pre-determined learning outcomes or goals for the experience, the decisions about which are out of your hands. For example, answers to questions like "Are there specific ideas, concepts, or understandings that the learners *must know*?" would constitute requirements.

And by **restraints**, we mean the conditions around the

experience that are out of your hands. For example, the amount of time you have, the number of participants in the group, and the physical setting in which the learning will take place are a few possible restraints.

With the requirements and restraints in mind, the choice often makes itself. Knowing the differences among lecturing, teaching, and facilitating fall largely on agency and active participation, you'll often find yourself seeing that lecturing is great when there are a lot of, or very limiting, requirements and restraints; and facilitating is perfect when you have more wiggle room in both areas.

And when in doubt, know that it's totally okay, and totally recommended, to mix it up: variety is the spice of life, and sometimes you won't figure out the best method to achieve a particular learning outcome until you've tried a few different ones.

EDUCATORS? LEARNERS? FACILITATION BLURS THE DIFFERENCE.

If you think back to our primer on facilitation, you'll recall that one of our favorite things about facilitation is how the idea-exchange is not unidirectional. That is, the educators are learners, and the learners are educators. In this chapter, we've used the language of Educator and Learner as an intentional detour from our typical Facilitator and Participant, because we want to make clear that sometimes the facilitator is the one learning and the participants are the ones teaching. That is, in every scenario above (lecturing, teaching, and facilitating), the person serving as Educator could be you or someone else.

What's more, the methods that facilitators and participants have at their disposal when serving as educators are one and the same: both facilitators and participants can choose to lecture, teach, or facilitate. If this is getting too abstract, let's consider a typical training moment that incorporates all three methods of achieving learning, being employed by both the facilitator and the participants:

Facilitator: "Why do you think we just did that activity?" *[Facilitating]*

Participant 1: "You wanted us to realize [...], because for our roles it's important to know [...]." *[Lecturing]*

Participant 2: to Participant 1 "Can you explain what you meant by [...]?" *[Facilitating]*

Participant 1: "I meant [...]. Is that more clear? Perhaps if you think of it like [...] it will help." *[Teaching]*

Facilitator: "Well said! And to put that another way, [...]." *[Teaching]*

Facilitator: "There is also another reason I wanted us to do that activity: [...]." *[Lecturing]*

And now, to put our Authors of a Book About Facilitation Caps back on, we want to leave you with this challenge: though it may be difficult, we believe it's possible to achieve the learning of pretty much any content through facilitation. And throughout this book, we hope to show you how.

Being Neutral

"You can't be neutral on a moving train."

- Howard Zinn

One of the most amusing things in life is when people start a sentence "No offense, but...." You know that not only are they about to say something (usually horrifyingly) offensive, but they think the caveat "no offense" somehow balances it back out to neutral. Or, as one of our favorite professors in grad school used to joke, when people say a terrible thing about another person, but add on the phrase "...bless their heart."

As facilitators, we often feel pressure to be seen as a neutral party in the room. In fact, neutrality is so idealized that we have about a dozen different phrases we deploy to ensure our neutral stance. To name a few, we have "objectively speaking," "most people would say," "not to pick sides," and "just playing the devil's advocate here" (often used when we want to masquerade as neutral, but still argue what we truly believe). We're concerned that if we are perceived as bringing our own biases into an educational setting, others will question the validity of what we have to say, or discredit it completely, chalking it up to an "of course you'd say that, you're [...]"-type prejudice.

Attempting to be neutral as a facilitator is about as possible as starting a sentence with "No offense, but..." and not offending anyone. We want to suggest that attempting neutrality isn't just unrealistic, it's unhelpful. Instead of expending energy on being perceived as neutral, you're better off (and your participants are better off) naming and working with the biases present—the biases we all have, and the societal pressures at large that are shaping the conversations in the room.

NEUTRALITY ISN'T NEUTRAL

Part of what is so appealing about "neutral" is the thought of some absolute truth, an unquestionable right or wrong. However, most of what we think of as neutral is really quite subjective, and generally just a majority opinion being masked as objective fact. First, let's ensure we're working from the same definition of neutral:

Neutral: absence of decided views, expression, or strong feeling (Google).

Let's take the most neutral, least subjective truth we can

muster, and break down what we're talking about when we say neutrality isn't neutral:

2 + 2 = 4.

No question that four being the sum of two and two is neutral, right? Well, that depends. Without questioning the factuality of the statement above, consider the following thoughts:

* Is everyone capable of determining that 2 + 2 = 4, or is there a set of beliefs or teachings necessary for one to come to that conclusion?

* Is everyone able to express why 2 + 2 = 4 in the same way, or with the same clarity?

* Will the statement 2 + 2 = 4 evoke the same feelings in everyone?

The symbols themselves are Hindu-Arabic, which are relatively widespread, and therefore may be thought of as neutral; but, as Sam learned when he was backpacking through Egypt and Jordan, in most of the shops he visited, 2 + 2 = ٤ (the original Arabic character for 4 looks surprisingly like a reversed Hindu-Arabic 3), which was confusing at first, to say the least. Even when folks understand the symbols of 2 and 4 the same way, asking several to express why 2 + 2 = 4 will likely get you several answers (from "because it does" to "ugh... I don't *do* math"), which brings us to the last point: math, though "objective" ("not influenced by personal feelings" [Google]), has a particularly subjective effect on people (it influences lots of personal feelings).

With those thoughts in mind, you might realize that the

answers to the above three bulleted questions are all "No." Does that mean that sum of two and two is not 4? Nope. It just means that even this "objective" case is not entirely neutral: it's not absent of decided views, expression, or strong feeling.

Now, considering the type of content you will be facilitating learning on, it probably won't strike you as too radical an idea to accept the following: achieving neutrality as a facilitator is impossible.

But that's okay.

BEING OPEN & HONEST, INSTEAD OF BEING "NEUTRAL"

As we've discussed above, neutrality isn't an achievable goal, and even if it were, we don't think it would be the one we'd want to aim for. But just because neutrality isn't possible, it doesn't mean you can't achieve some of the goals that neutrality espouses.

Being "neutral" (scare quotes intended) is often one of two things: (1) a person intentionally trying to present a space as open-minded and free of judgment; or (2) a person ignoring their own biases and dominant cultural biases and presenting them as objective. The latter is pernicious, and too prickly for us to get into in this book[1]. And we hope to show you that your best bet in accomplishing the first is, as counterintuitive as it seems, by being open and honest about

---

1 If it's something you want to dive into, this book is part of a larger forthcoming book called *A Guide to Facilitation: The Social Justice Advocate's Handbook*, which has an entire section dedicated to this. And in the meantime, we have some resources on the official website for this book that might tide you over.

how closed-minded and judgmental we actually are (bless our hearts).

By openly and honestly naming our biases, and the cultural biases we've unknowingly internalized or brought into a space, we are most able to create a space where folks are genuinely able to share their perspectives, explore difficult subjects, and be honest themselves. Here are a few tips:

* **If something is politically charged, address the political charge.** Most social justice topics are couched in a lot of different belief systems: political, religious, personal, and beyond. Recognizing that there are multiple perspectives from which to view any one issue allows others to be more comfortable adding theirs to the conversation.

* **Allow participants to share their opinions even when (especially when) they differ from yours.** You have biases about the material you're facilitating, and so do the participants in the room. Don't cut folks off simply because their biases are different from yours, and let them know they can share freely in the space, but...

* **Recognize the goals of the learning space, and highlight them when highlighting your and others' biases.** If the goal of a training is to reduce racism, there is a clear bias against thoughts, ideas, and understandings that are rooted in or reinforce racism. Your bias as the facilitator, then, is an anti-racist one, and calling out racist bias (yours and others') is key to achieving the goals of the training.

* **Be selective about when you share your opinion or experiences.** Your opinion, will often create a climate where the "neutral" is similar to you, disproportionate to other people's sharing. Know your voice carries this

weight every time you decide to weigh in.

Creating a space where people can share differing opinions, and where the judgment of others and you as the facilitator won't impede that, is an admirable goal. It's one we celebrate and encourage. To do this, we do not need to present a facade of neutrality with our words, but use actions to level the playing field. In the next few chapters, we will provide you with a bunch of tools that do just that. *And no offense, but you're gonna need 'em.*

How to
Read a Group

"Listen and be led."

- L.M. Heroux

When Sam first started performing stand-up comedy, someone gave him a piece of advice: good comedians aren't the ones who know how to talk the best, but the ones who know how to listen. Sam had no idea what to do with this advice until almost a year later when he started facilitating group discussions. The best comedians and the best facilitators, in this case, have an important thing in common: they know how to read and respond to a group. And to do that, we have to know how to listen.

Let's start with the listening, then get into how it helps with the reading.

READING A GROUP MEANS LEARNING HOW TO LISTEN

You may be thinking, "Are they going to tell me I need to be an *active listener*? [commence eye roll]" because so often any conversation about listening turns into a conversation about active listening (or the often blurry distinction between "listening" and "hearing"). If your eyes are rolling, you can safely return them to a non-rolled position. While active listening is wonderful, what we're talking about here is less nuanced and even more important: great facilitators spend more time listening than talking.

And, for the sake of this chapter, that's it. To read a group, the first step is to listen more and talk less.

Now, don't get too far ahead of us. While it's easy in theory, not talking is—for some of us more than others—a near-impossible task in practice. Nerves, good intentions, and fear of quiet can equally demolish any chance we have of listening more than talking. There are several things you can do to improve your odds of listening.

During Sam's undergraduate experience as an orientation leader, his mentor Kelly came up with a mnemonic W.H.A.L.E. for facilitators to use while leading group discussions. Used after a facilitator asked a question of the group, the goal of W.H.A.L.E. (which stood for, if Sam's memory serves him, Wait, Hesitate, Ask [again], Listen, then Explain) was to prevent facilitators from answering their own questions, and subsequently dominating the discussion they were there to lead. You'll notice the first two steps in the

W.H.A.L.E. acronym are "Wait" and "Hesitate." That's right: two parts of the five-part solution were *don't do anything.*

Being silent and letting yourself pause as people think about questions or where they need to go next is a risk. It can feel intimidating, uncomfortable, and vulnerable. Sometimes a group will laugh awkwardly, look around at each other, or just stare you down. Every second can feel like an hour, and you might have a voice inside your head yelling the answer to the question you just asked, begging you to fill the void. Resist that urge, and you have a shot at reading your group.

If you are like us, and find it difficult to listen to silence, and vomit words all over your participants (ALL OF THE WORDS), here are a few pointers that will help:

1. Develop a system that works for you. What is something that can keep you from clouding the air with words? For Sam, the acronym W.H.A.L.E. helped immeasurably in the beginning. He would ask a question, then in his head recite "Wait...Hesitate..." and usually by then someone else would have broken the silence. Maybe counting works for you. Maybe you know all the words to Poe's "The Raven" and you want recite those. Whatever. Just have something you can run through in your mind to quiet the urge to talk out loud.

2. Trust the system. This might be the only time you'll ever see us type these words, being folks who generally don't trust—and are actively working to subvert—systems of control. But in this case, it's a benevolent system; this is not The Matrix. When you're in a situation where you feel like it's your responsibility to talk, a second of listening feels like an hour. It's easy to throw it all away and just ramble. Hell, we still do it. Try not to. Trust the system, Neo (take the blue pill).

3. Allow others to crumble first. There aren't many laws when it comes to groups of human beings, but there is one that has never failed us: if you don't talk, someone else will. Sometimes you have to wait a seemingly excruciatingly long time (like two, or maybe even three whole seconds), but someone else *will* crumble first if you allow them to. The more you experience this happening, the more fun it becomes. Biting our tongues through awkward silences has actually become one of our favorite things—an enjoyable discomfort, like a *Fear Factor* challenge (only in that case, it would probably involve biting some other thing's tongue).

4. Just stop talking for a bit. Like we said before, there isn't anything philosophical or fancy about this version of "learning how to listen." Just use your ears more, and other people will feel more compelled to use their mouths.

When we were discussing this subject, Meg shared she has never regretted being too silent during a training she was facilitating. On the other hand, there have been a boat load of times she's walked away from a training thinking, "Mhmm, I did too much talking there," and that motivates her to keep quiet next time. Share the airtime.

NOW THAT YOU'RE LISTENING: READ THE GROUP

Consider for a moment the experience of someone reading a pop-up book to you. There is so much more to a pop-up book than just the words on the page—there are movements, visuals, and the tone of the narrator. And there are also the words on the page. All of these elements blend together to tell you a more vibrant, more complete story. Now imagine the pop-up book is also a choose-your-own-adventure style book, where at different stages you, as the listener, are prompted to alter the story itself.

Reading a group of people is like having a choose-your-own-adventure pop-up book read to you. Every element—from the words on the page to the tone of the narrator—is important, and if you listen to each, you will get the most complete story of your group. Let's clarify how these elements apply to reading a group, starting with the most obvious.

The Words On the Page

There is much more to a pop-up book than the words, but the words are still important. Similarly important are the actual words you get from your group. This is square one of reading a group: directly asking people how they feel about something, then listening to them when they tell you.

There are two parts here, and it's crucial we do both of them: the asking and the listening. If you've ever been to a comedy show, you've no doubt experienced a comedian directly asking a group how they're feeling ("How's everyone doing tonight?"). And if you're lucky, you've experienced a great comedian who actually listens to the response, instead of just moving on with whatever they planned to say next ("Whoa—I heard that groan in the front row. Sounded like someone got punched in the gut by the cold outside."). If a group knows you're actually listening, they'll be more likely to speak up.

While facilitating a training, we can do the same thing. We can ask questions like "How is everyone feeling about…" or "Show of hands if…" or "Nod if…" or (Sam's personal favorite) "Snaps if…" (because he was a bad snapper as a kid, but is now awesome at it, and clearly over-proud). The words your participants use when they give you answers, when they tell you how they are feeling, or what they are struggling with, are the first cue to use when reading them as a group.

Here are some ways you can get more words on the page:

1. **Entry surveys.** If possible, have the group fill out a little survey before your training to get a sense of their wants, experiences, dispositions, and identities. This is part of what we call "front loading." Demographic data of the group are words on the page. Questions they have for you before the training starts are words on the page.

2. **Ask the group check-in questions throughout the workshop.** Ask them what they think about things. Ask them how they feel. Ask them to rephrase points you made, or someone else in the room made. Ask them to reflect back on the first half of a workshop aloud. Process the process. Ask them whatever you need to know— just, you know, shut up once you do (see above section).

We love index card check-ins. You can pass out index cards and use them to check in with the group whenever you need to know what they're thinking, but you're not sure they will say it aloud. For example, we use them after intense activities to give participants a chance to write down how they are feeling, then we will read them at random and allow other participants to nod or snap if they're feeling similarly. Index cards are a low-risk, in-the-moment, anonymous way to get more words on the page.

3. Use responses to questions and activities as launching points for discussions. Nothing will tell you more about where someone is on a subject than their responses to your discussion questions. A great prompt to see if someone understands something is "Recap what we just talked about in your own words." And after someone answers a question, you can present what they said to the rest of the group (e.g., "Did anyone else have that same thought?") to get a sense of where they are with the material being discussed.

THE MOVING PARTS: EXAMINING BODY LANGUAGE AND ENERGY

Just like the structures that come out of the pop-up book as you turn the page, examining the moving parts of your group can add to your impressions of the story. When we think of moving parts, we think primarily of body language and energy.

Body Language

The way people are sitting, where they're looking, and what they're doing with their hands are all important parts of the story. Body language is the sum total of all the non-verbal cues you can discern from a person or group. Reading body language is nuanced, and we are not going to get too into the depth of it here, but Google "Body Language TED Talks" or find a good book if you want to learn more. For our purposes, here are a few non-verbal cues we look out for:

1. Crossing arms and legs might mean someone is feeling threatened, or needs to put up their guard. In a training, this might be because they are feeling targeted, or just uncomfortable with the subject.

2. Physically turning away from someone, whether it's another member of the group or you as the facilitator, might indicate someone is attempting to disengage from that person.

3. No eye contact, or staring off into the distance, might mean that someone is bored, but it also could mean someone is processing. Processing is good. Bored is less good.

4. Phone usage can feel like a personal affront, like an intentional way to ignore what you are saying. When someone isn't paying attention to you and is instead more interested in what is happening in their lap or on their little screen, it can be hard not to feel like they are checked out.

For all of the above, the best way to understand what's going on is to set clear intentions in the beginning of a training (e.g., "We expect everyone to engage in the discussion"), and then check in with the participants if you sense their body language is telling you something otherwise. Occasionally, you'll be misreading a person's nonverbal cues, and a verbal check-in can clarify what you're seeing. Cell phone use, for example, use can be more compulsive than purposeful at times, in which case you're best off not to take it personally.

Energy

Energy is about movement as much as it is about a lack of movement. If you turned a page of a pop-up book, and nothing poked out, you'd be quick to notice there was a problem, and tug at the right part of the page to fix it. Low energy in a group, while sometimes less obvious, can also be shifted with the right tug.

When a group is energized, it doesn't necessarily mean that they are dancing around and laughing (though if that's the energy you accomplish in your trainings, count us in). An energized group is engaged in the material, attentive to whomever is speaking, and actively learning from the training. In reading the energy of a group, there are a couple of things to keep in mind: (1) How long are you going to be together? (2) What were they doing before the trainings and what will be happening after?

If you're working with a group for longer than an hour, you need to be sensitive to their attention spans. Even with less than an hour you can quickly lose people, but with longer trainings it will be more and more important to make intentional decisions to positively influence the energy of the group. With long trainings, managing the energy of the group can be as important to accomplishing the goals as knowing the material you are discussing.

And what the group was doing before you were together, and what they're doing after, can be just as important to their energy as the actual training you are in together. If they just came from a draining, exhausting, or boring experience, keep that in mind. If it's early in the morning and people are just getting caffeine in their bodies, keep that in mind. Or if it's the end of the day on Friday, and people are excited to be done with their week, keep that in mind.

Beyond that, energy can be a hard thing to explain. For us, knowing the energy of a group is sometimes simply a feeling in our gut that says "These people are *into this*" or "These people are *about to pass out*." Other times, you can tell the energy is low by the tone in participants' voices (if everyone is starting to sound flat) or a lack of effort in transitioning from one activity to the next (everyone groans as they stand up, or turn a page).

If you're noticing the group's energy is low, hope is not lost.

A few tips for recharging your group's batteries:

1. Take a break and encourage people to get up, walk around, and stretch. If your training is a long one (several hours plus), take 15 minutes. If it's a short training, take five. If you've ever been falling asleep in a class and knew if you just stood up and stretched how much more awake you'd be, you'll understand how helpful it can be.

2. Rearrange the room and the people in it. Switching the configuration of the room can create new energy: swap the seating arrangement (e.g., if you were in a classroom style, change it to an open circle, or small pods) and ask participants to sit by someone new.

3. Change the type of interaction you're using to engage your group. If you've been lecturing a lot, move to facilitating a conversation, or teaching a topic where there can be more back and forth between you and the group. Put people in small groups or in pairs to get everyone participating.

4. Consider bringing movement into the training itself. For example, instead of asking if people agree or disagree, have them show you: make a values statement and have the participants stand up and organize themselves on a spectrum from strongly agree to strongly disagree.

TONE AND QUALITY OF VOICE: THE MESSAGE BEHIND THE WORDS

How someone says something can be as important as what they're saying. One of our favorite examples of this is the famous "I never said she stole my money" inflections. This sentence can be emphasized to mean seven different things, by changing which word is **emphasized**:

I never said she stole my money.
[someone else may have]
I **never** said she stole my money.
[I didn't say it and how dare you accuse me of doing so]
I never **said** she stole my money.
[but she tots did]
I never said **she** stole my money.
[but someone else did, and that person is a jerk]
I never said she **stole** my money.
[I gave it to her, just, not, entirely willingly]
I never said she stole **my** money.
[but she stole someone's, and for that she's a jerk]
I never said she stole my **money**.
[she stole my heart. I gave her the money. I <3 jerks.]

In facilitation, try to pay as much attention to the how as the what. And, as always, if you're unsure of what someone is trying to convey with their tone, check in. Find your own style of checking in and figure out what feels natural to you.

The best "checking in" advice we can give here is to name what you observe (e.g., "So I heard you say that she stole your money...") and then explain why you're circling back to it ("...but how you said it made me feel unclear about why you wanted to share that with us. Can you tell me a bit more?"). It never hurts to ask someone to rephrase something before you react, to make sure you're reacting to what they actually want you to be reacting to.

CHOOSE THEIR OWN ADVENTURE

If you've never read a choose your own adventure book, the premise is simple. At different points in the story, the author gives the reader the ability to decide where it'll go next ("Turn to page 13 if you get this reference; turn to page 89 if you want to see Sam and Meg stop using this analogy"). In reading a group during a workshop, it's great if you can create opportunities where they have the ability to choose where the story goes next. Nothing will tell you what a group wants more than giving them control over where the training goes next.

The simplest way to achieve this is by asking. You could take a vote ("Raise your hand if you want to spend 5 more minutes on this") or ask for submissions ("What should we talk about for these last 5 minutes?"). Asking where the group wants go to is also a helpful component of frontloading, if you have the chance to hear from the group before they form.

Another way to let them choose their own adventure is to listen when they're trying to tell you they already have. If folks keep asking questions about a certain subject, they're choosing their own adventure. Cover that subject. If nobody seems engaged by whatever you're talking about, ditto. If someone seems triggered, angry, or confused, that likely warrants switching to a different page and addressing those concerns.

Remember, facilitation isn't about plotting out a course

and etching it in stone, but about letting the winds and currents nudge you around on your journey toward a common goal.

Both/And > Or/But

"That's what careless words do. They make people love you a little less."

- Arundhati Roy

et's consider two situations. In both, someone is facilitating a training with a group, and their goal is to help the group understand humanity's effect on global climate change. One participant is struggling with the material. For this example, let's do our best to empathize with that participant.

In the first situation, the participant in the training who is struggling pushes back. They say, "I don't understand how you can think the planet is warming. We just had a terrible blizzard last week." The facilitator, confident that the material being covered is factually true, sensitively responds, "I appreciate you sharing your perspective. A lot of people share that concern, but extreme weather is actually a symptom of climate change."

Now consider an alternative situation, where everything is the same, except for one word being changed: the facilitator responds, "I appreciate you sharing your perspective. A lot of people share that concern, **and** extreme weather is actually a symptom of climate change."

You may have already had a feeling in your gut in response to that simple word change: the feeling of "and" and the feeling of "but" can be dramatically different. If you felt it, then your gut has already taught you what this chapter is all about. If the message didn't make it to your gut just yet, no worries—we'll do our best to work our way from your head down.

AND VS. BUT: UNPACKING THE DIFFERENCE

"And" and "But" serve similar functions grammatically. And, generally speaking, we can exchange one for the other without noticing much of a difference in meaning. But when disagreeing with someone, the difference between "and" and "but" grows to a canyon.

Whenever someone makes a statement, connecting your response to theirs with "and" builds on what they said; connecting your response to theirs with "but" negates what they said. "And" recognizes their truth, and adds yours on top of or alongside it; "But" negates their truth, and replaces it with yours.

"Meg is wonderful, *but* she smells bad." Meg might be wonderful, but that is diminished by the fact that she smells bad. "Meg is wonderful, *and* she smells bad." In this sentence, Meg's wonderfulness isn't diminished by her odor—heck, it might even be part of her charm ("Meg is so busy being wonderful she ain't got *time* to shower—I respect that."). What we're doing with the "And" is allowing these two ideas to have their own merit, to exist alongside one another, instead of putting them on opposite ends of an ideological tug of war (the classic hot-button controversy of "wonderful" vs. "smell bad" you're always hearing about on cable news).

MANIFESTING POLAR BEARS

Facilitation requires so much attention to so many competing things, it can be easy for us to accidentally create a throwdown we had no intention of throwing down. Sometimes, something as small as saying "But" when you could have said "And" will trigger a fight or flight reflex in a participant, where you turn them into a hyper-protective mama bear whose cub is her idea. We'll call this manifesting polar bears.

If you want to steer clear of polar bears, your best bet is to avoid poles. We are really good at internalizing two ideas as competing, polar opposites, when often they're better understood as two distinct ideas, and not actually in competition at all.

Do your best to be intentional about which ideas, or what material, you're discussing are actually polar opposites, and which can happily coexist.

But/Or Create a Hunger Games of Ideas

If there really is one absolute truth--a winning idea that needs to emerge as victorious--creating dichotomies and forcing people to choose one concept over another is necessary. Responding to participants' statements with "but" and "or" are great ways to create that competition.

Sometimes allowing for multiple perspectives won't help. It may create more confusion than clarity, or the ambiguity is occasionally too difficult for participants to hold, and without anything concrete to anchor them, all the learning drops out. We understand this. We simply encourage you to pick your ideological battle royales.

"What you just said might be true, or everything we know might be a lie and our universe is really a simulation being run by some super-computer of an advanced civilization."

And/Both Create a Sandbox Where Everyone Can Play

One of the best things about facilitation is bringing learning out of a bunch of individuals, and enabling them to share what they know with one another. Most ideas can play nicely with other ideas if we allow them to.

When it's clear that the learning being shared can add to the learning you're hoping to accomplish as a facilitator, we encourage you to "And" relentlessly. If you notice a false dichotomy that participants are struggling with, a carefully placed "both" can keep them from flinging sand in one another's eyes.

*"Folks, may I suggest something? Perhaps the leaders of the advanced civilization controlling our universe are **both** 'a huge pile of jerks' for taking away the dinosaurs **and** 'benevolent*

all-healing gods' for giving us guacamole."

HOW BOTH/AND LOOKS IN THE MOMENT

Hopefully you don't need convincing that multiple truths and realities exist—about any and every concept—even when they seem to contradict each other. And maybe the above helped you recognize the power you have to create space for these multiple realities, or to demolish them, all with your choice of conjunction[1]. Having the ability to identify the *"But" statements* that can be *"And" statements* is an important skill. As soon as you're comfortable with that distinction, you can move into choosing your language intentionally, and, in turn, helping participants understand that multiple truths and realities can exist together. Here are a few things to think about that might help you do just that.

YOUR REALITY BEING TRUE DOESN'T MEAN MY REALITY ISN'T

It's easy for us to fall into the trap of believing that our truth is dependent upon it being universally true. Sam is constantly arguing that the entirety of *The Matrix* trilogy has merit, and has a hard time believing that when literally every person he talks to thinks the latter two films are worthless. He can be right (i.e., all three films can add worth to his life), and everyone else can be right (i.e., the second two movies are, to them, a festering waste of film, money, time, and Keanu Reeves). Both parties are right, and Sam is delusional.

---

1 *Conjunction Junction, what's your function? I've got two real choices, and one will get me far: Protect participants' realities, or destroy and leave them scarred.*

We see this come up again and again in facilitation: if my reality is this way then your reality can't be that way. "If I am experiencing what you said as problematic, and you didn't, we can't both be right." Instead of discussing the core of the issue, we talk about who is "really right" as if there is an absolute reality we are close to, and need to find. The Both/And concept allows us to stop having that conversation and move into having the next phase of the conversation, which is "tell me about your reality, and then I can tell you about mine." This is particularly important with social justice concepts, when you're attempting to affirm many different types of experiences and understandings of self, some of which are less part of the dominant narrative than others.

AND MY REALITY BEING TRUE DOESN'T MEAN IT'S TRUE FOR YOU

At some point, far too late into his adult life, Sam realized that he can appreciate all three *Matrix* films, while everyone else hates them. In fact, he now celebrates that he might be the only person in the world who likes all three films ("More metal plug-shaped Keanu Reeve nipples for me.").

Creating space for Both/And means recognizing that disagreeing is okay, healthy, even desirable, and can lead to learning for everyone. As a facilitator, your first hurdle is getting over your own But/Or thinking when it comes to something a participant says. Your second hurdle (often higher, more wibbly-wobbly, and likely to send you sprawling) is helping participants get over their But/Or thinking in response to what other participants say.

A phrase we use, that you are welcome to think of as the penicillin of facilitator interjections, is "Thanks for sharing your perspective. It's always nice to see how many different perspectives people have about this." Then, when another participant shares a contradicting or directly retaliatory view, you can use it again. "And thanks for sharing *your* perspective! It's always nice to see how many different perspectives people have about this." And you can rinse and repeat until your participants evolve into an anti-confrontational resistant superbug.

Enabling participants to have coexisting—instead of competing—unique perspectives amongst one another is as important as recognizing when their perspective and your perspective can coexist.

IMPORTANT BOTH/AND CONCEPTS

There are innumerable situations in which Both/And will come in handy. Instead, we're going to highlight a few of the most easy-to-But/Or concepts we can think of, and all of them come from a fountain of perpetual controversy: the perspective, process, and goal that is social justice. It is our hope that in seeing how these highly divisive concepts are unified, you'll be able to extrapolate this out to just about any situation you might experience in your facilitation.

YOU CAN BE BOTH PRIVILEGED AND OPPRESSED

We often talk about privilege and oppression as if they were the two positions of a light switch: you can either be oppressed, or privileged—no in between, no other options. This, like all Both/And-able concepts that are But/Or-ed, creates unnecessary conflict, demolishes nuance, and prevents understanding and empathy. Every person has many identities, and experiences those identities in unique ways, depending on location, time, and the rest of who they are.

Not only can a single person experience both oppression *and* privilege, most of us do! Being able to accept and present that reality, being both privileged and oppressed, helps others see the complexity of both issues, and creates some wiggle room for a productive dialogue.

YOU CAN BE DOING GOOD (OR TRYING TO) AND CAUSING HARM

We often struggle when our intentions don't align with outcomes, and participants in a training will be the first to latch onto just that. As facilitators, it's easy to focus on the harm someone causes, and we might be able to enable more learning for everyone if we also acknowledge the good (whether manifested or intended). And we, as facilitators, often do the same thing. For example, if we are silencing, forgetting, or even purposefully excluding particular marginalized voices, perspectives, and identities from the conversation, this *is* doing harm (it's reinforcing the erasure and marginalization these perspectives experience in society), *and* it might be doing good (we might recognize that trying to talk about *everything all at once* will lead to confusion, and instead focus on accomplishing a small, specific win instead). Sam may be doing a great job facilitating a workshop about lesbian, gay, and bisexual identities and completely ignore (or not leave time to discuss) asexuality. Whether intentional or not, this may cause harm while simultaneously doing good: participants may have a vastly more comprehensive understanding of LGB identities but have no more understanding, empathy, or connection to asexual identities.

As facilitators, we have to make choices like this all the time. It happens when we decide what we are going to be discussing or not covering, what concepts we are prioritizing and what concepts we just may not get to. These are difficult choices, and many of us are aware that we're doing some amount of harm (even if it's just in way of not doing good), *while* we're doing good. Keep this in mind, and use it as your source of empathy, when helping participants recognize they are often doing the same thing.

KEEPING YOUR BUT OUT OF CONVERSATIONS

This concept can be difficult to unsee now that you've seen it—like many others in the book (we hope!). It undermines a foundational component of our communication that we may not have realized we were communicating. You might, for a short while, find yourself stumbling over basic sentences in conversations with others (e.g., Someone asks "How are you?" and you reply "I'm well, but today—oh no. Is that an and? Hm... 'and' today...? Hold on a sec! Can I try again?"), to the utter *confusion* of those others. In fact, it's not uncommon for us to get an email from someone we trained, days or weeks after the training, like the following email Sam received:

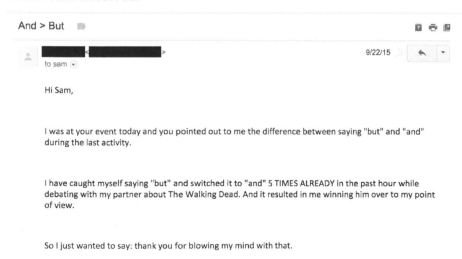

And > But

9/22/15

to sam

Hi Sam,

I was at your event today and you pointed out to me the difference between saying "but" and "and" during the last activity.

I have caught myself saying "but" and switched it to "and" 5 TIMES ALREADY in the past hour while debating with my partner about The Walking Dead. And it resulted in me winning him over to my point of view.

So I just wanted to say: thank you for blowing my mind with that.

We understand. This concept had—and has—a similar effect on us.

You might also find yourself glowing with pride when you pepper in an "and" where previously you would have un-wittingly inserted your "but." We're guilty here, too.

We're not sure which one leads to more social awkward-ness: the cursing yourself for saying "but," or the "my kid is going to Harvard" pride when you nail the "and." What we can say for sure is that both are likely to lead the other per-son in the conversation to think you've had way too much caffeine.

This technique is something that will take time to utilize without awkwardness, *and* that's okay! Curse yourself, pat yourself on the back, do neither or both, and keep reading. Now that you've stumbled upon the ground-shaking glory that is "and is greater than but," you're ready for something even more powerful: the "Yes, And..." rule.

The"Yes, And..." Rule

"Say yes, and you'll figure it out afterwards."

- Tina Fey

There is an indispensable rule of improv comedy that also works wonders with facilitation: the "Yes, And..." Rule. Any improviser you meet will know it, and many will explain it to you with glee. At this point, the rule is less well known in the facilitator world, and we hope to change that. Using the "Yes, And..." Rule (YAR!) in your facilitation allows multiple things to be true at the same time, it allows you to disagree without destroying someone's reality, and it encourages participants to add their voices to the learning.

The way it works is simple: if someone says something, you agree and build onto it. Or you can think of it in the negative: when someone says something, *you don't disagree*, but instead find ways to see their truth, and add yours to it.

In improv, this leads to more energetic, complex, and funny scenes. Imagine a scene with two improvisers, where one person wants it to be set in orbit, and the other person is imagining it will take place on a beach. The first improviser might say, "It sure is cold out here in SPACE!" The second improviser can say, "No, it's not, but it sure is hot on this BEACH." (Womp womp...) Or, they can YAR and say "Yeah! And I thought we were spending the day at beach, so I'm bummed I only packed my bikini. But good thing I have this SPF 100, considering we're FLYING DIRECTLY INTO THE SUN."

The YAR can be tricky in improv, where we often have a particular narrative in mind and don't see how easily we can add it on top of someone else's. And it can be even trickier in facilitation.

You have a goal, or an intended outcome for the time with your group, and to get to that goal, people need to say certain things. Improvisers only have the simple goal of making people laugh, though that might not be *too* different from our goals as facilitators, which we'll explain at the end of the chapter.

First, let's make sure we're on the same page with what this rule is, isn't, and why we love it so.

WHY NO "NO"?

The simplest reason is that "No" often shuts down dialogue. If it's important to engage the people you're working with in dialogue, to open up the conversation for more exploration and more idea sharing, a "No" in the room might signal to everyone that they should keep silent.

Think of the contribution a participant makes to a discussion as children's artwork: it may be crude, incomplete, lacking in expertise, unrepresentative of reality, and sometimes downright offensive, *and* there is almost always something beautiful about it. If you tell a kid "This sucks. You suck," they'll never paint again, they'll never get better, and it's simply not true: just the fact that they are painting is courageous and beautiful. Saying "No" to a participant can feel like telling a kid their painting sucks.

That's not nice. Let's play nice with others.

If you want people to share their ideas with the group, you need to treat them with the same tenderness, understanding, and sensitivity that you'd treat a kid who shows you their (terrible, ugly, *is that racist? I think it's racist*) paintings: acknowledge the good you see, encourage them to keep working, and maybe share with them something you've been working on. The YAR is a super easy trick to do all of that in the moment.

How "No" looks in action

"No" shuts down someone's thought without inviting further feedback. Consider the following exchange:

Participant: Abstinence-only sex education is the best way to prevent teen pregnancies.

Facilitator: No, that's incorrect. Comprehensive sex education is best for preventing unwanted teen pregnancies, and abstinence-only education has more negative than positive effects[1].

In this instance, the participant is likely to either disengage or start arguing—neither of which is ideal. And we've forced this ultimatum before learning so much: we don't know why the participant believes what they believe (e.g., what source?); we don't know why it felt important to them to share (e.g., are they motivated to lower teen pregnancy rate, or are they more motivated to end comprehensive sex education; and in both cases, why?); and we don't know how other people in the room feel about what the participant said (e.g., is this participant the only one who believes this, or is the facilitator the only one who doesn't?).

Knowing all of the above information would allow the facilitator to connect with the participant and have a more productive conversation. They could enter the conversation through a point of connection, and then create a space where the more accurate/inclusive/sensitive information is learned. And even if they don't use the information in that moment, it will offer them more perspective in the future—it's one of the many moments in a training when the facilitator can learn from a participant.

If the facilitator's goal in this moment is to help the participant see that abstinence-only education is not an effective way to prevent teen pregnancies, then creating an argument, or pushing the person out of the discussion, won't likely do this. The facilitator can attempt to teach the partic-

---

1 Something we can't do in a live discussion: cite our source. For those curious, many studies show that abstinence-only education does nothing to lower the rate of teen pregnancies or delay teenage sexual activity, and a federally-funded survey of these sex education policies has shown that they may make teens more resistant to using contraceptives when they do become sexually active: http://bit.ly/UTMaose

ipant, but facilitation works wonders to achieve learning in controversial situations, as we discussed before. And in this particular moment, YAR is the key to creating more learning, instead of more controversy.

WALK THE PLANK INTO YAR

A lot of concepts in this book don't feel natural at first. If a participant says something you're uncomfortable with, or that you don't think is right, it's tough to say the "Yes" part of the "Yes, And..." Rule. We get that, and we experience it on a regular basis, and even with all that discomfort and difficulty, we are still diehard "Yes, And..."-ers. Being a YARer comes with a set of expectations.

If someone presents a reality to you, you will validate that reality. If someone shares their opinion with you, you will validate their opinion. You'll validate their thoughts and beliefs—however ridiculous, offensive, or just plain *different* they may be from your own (or from "reality")—even if it just means you'll validate that they *have them*. You are willing to accept that someone else's worldview is different from yours, or from the "ideal" in the sense of the training goals, and that you can build on their reality instead of demolishing it.

This requires discomfort (both yours, and your participants'). It requires courage (you have to be willing to explore things you may not have wanted to, nor been prepared to, explore). It requires patience (it is often the least direct path to learning). It requires you to harness the power of subtle language (particularly the difference between "But" and "And"). And it requires trust (in the process of facilitation, because though indirect, the learning that's achieved will be more powerful).

A kid will show you their painting of your house—where the trees are blue and the people in the house are yellow and the sky is green and you're not sure (but you're pretty sure) the house looks like it's on fire—and you'll say "Yes! That's a painting. And I love that you made it, even if I would have painted a version of our house that wasn't a dystopian hellscape burning down with us inside."

How "yes" looks in action

When you're in total disagreement with someone, starting with "Yes" creates a healthier dynamic. Think back to the previous chapter on the energetic difference between "But" and "And." When you say to someone, "Yes, and..." what you're also saying is "I hear you. I see what you're saying. Your voice is valued."

Even if what you say next is totally different from what they think, they'll at least feel heard. For facilitation to work, it is important for participants to know they are being heard. This enables discussions to foster more genuine curiosity, instead of predatory listening[2], where folks are just waiting for their turn to attack an idea that's put forth, instead of truly considering its merit.

The YAR also helps you model one of the prickliest parts of great facilitation, which we'll discuss in the last chapter

---

2 Meg first heard the phrase "predatory listening" at a keynote given by Caprice Hollins at the Association of Experiential Educators International Conference in 2015. Caprice cited Peggy McIntosh as being the one who introduced her to the concept. It's a phrase to describe something a lot of us have experienced (or practiced) that so perfectly sums it up. We love the phrase so much we knew we had to include it in the book somewhere, and it fits well here (as well as it would have fit in so many other chapters).

of this book: it will enable participants not to see you as the sole expert who has all the answers, and instead recognize the knowledge and expertise we all bring with us to any setting.

Let's revisit the example from earlier, this time replacing the "No" with a "Yes, and..."

Participant: Abstinence-only sex education is the best way to prevent teen pregnancies.

Facilitator: Yes, it totally makes sense that teaching kids to avoid having sex would lead to them not having unwanted pregnancies, and I had that same belief when I first started doing sex education. Are there any reasons you all can think of that might lead abstinence-only sex education students to having more unwanted pregnancies, instead of fewer?

The "And" we used here was one of past-tense agreement, which, in at least Sam's case, is totally honest. As a sex educator, he's able to draw on his first reactions to sex ed, one of which had him in agreement with that participant ("Of course encouraging kids not to have sex will lead to fewer unwanted pregnancies," said Younger Sam).

The second dimension of the "And" we have above is one that asks others, and even the first participant, to provide their own evidence to the alternative in a safe way. After hearing these perspectives (and, usually, waiting for a few keywords), the facilitator can then summarize with the same sentiment they led with in the "No" version of this example earlier. And the facilitator can do this in a way that doesn't shut down the first participant, but uses what the participant said as part of the learning—and best of all, the facilitator is doing it in a way that models growth, changes of perspectives, and being willing to learn tough things ("Of course *only* encouraging kids to not have sex will lead to more unwanted pregnancies," says Right Now Sam).

It's not always a "Yes" and an "And"

The sentiment of the rule is more important than the specific language. You can YAR without ever uttering a "Yes," or an "And," and still have the same effect on the group.

To be as flexible as possible, let's replace the exact language with the two sentiments that we're hoping you'll evoke in your language: (1) I hear your perspective; and (2) I'd like to invite you to witness another perspective.

Instead of saying *"Yes, and..."* you might find yourself saying *"I hear what you're saying, and..."*, or *"I appreciate you sharing that perspective. Would anyone like to add to it?"*, or any other combination of sentiments 1 and 2 above. There are countless ways you can utilize the YAR; we want you to know that "Yes, And..." is just one of them.

You can likely already see how nifty a tool we have at our disposal with YAR. You might also be thinking, "Wait. Above, you said there were so many more things we could have learned by not saying 'No,' but the facilitator didn't really learn them in that example." Good catch, astute reader. (Five points to Gryffindor!) Now let's look at how digging for more information might have played out.

YAR for more Information

YARing can be an effective way to curiously dig for more information. Finding out where your participants are coming from, who else shares a belief, and what concepts or theories are at play supporting their beliefs are all important. The more information you have, the more you can connect ideas together to facilitate learning.

Revisiting our initial scenario, let's YAR to find out a little more about what our participants are thinking:

Participant: Abstinence-only sex education is the best way to prevent teen pregnancies.

Facilitator: I appreciate you sharing your perspective, and I bet there are other people who feel the same way. Would anyone else who believes that abstinence-only sex education is the best way to prevent teen pregnancies care to share more about why they believe that?

In this deployment of the YAR, rather than putting it back on the participant who first shared the comment, we've used it to invite others into the discussion and to provide additional perspective on that comment. This lets others who agree also feel heard, and lets the first participant off the hook from feeling compelled to defend themselves (a feeling we're trying to avoid).

But sometimes you do want to know more about what that particular person is thinking. Maybe you suspect they are the only one that holds that perspective, or, more likely, the only one who may be willing to speak more to that perspective. Here's how that might look:

Participant: Abstinence-only sex education is the best way to prevent teen pregnancies.

Facilitator: I appreciate you sharing your perspective, and there are a lot of possible reasons for that perspective to make sense. Can you tell me more about why you believe that abstinence-only sex education is the best way to prevent teen pregnancies?

It is important when digging for more information that

the person feels that you're genuinely curious about why the hold that belief of perspective. Without that genuine curiosity they may feel attacked or like you're about to use whatever they say against them. If you can't muster a genuine curiosity, we advise against this deployment of the YAR.

PICK THE CHOCOLATE OUT OF THEIR TRAIL MIX

The different examples we've covered so far have been when our participant has made a short statement we disagree with. If you've ever had who we in the biz sophistically label a "talker" in your training, you know that isn't always how it goes down. Often, participants will make less of a "statement" and more of a word-vomity, tangled-spaghetti rant of opinions, "facts," and/or fortune telling—sometimes all three merged together presented as "I'm just saying how things are."

When a participant makes a statement that is more expansive, we can have more to work with right off the bat, and that's where picking the chocolate out of their trail mix comes in.

When you are eating trail mix out of someone else's bowl, it's rude to pick out the good stuff (the chocolate, gummies, chunks of sugar, etc.) and leave all the peanuts and giant brown crunchy discs behind, sad and lonely. This is decidedly *not* rude in facilitation. If someone says a bunch of things, and most of them are anything but sweet, pick out and repeat the sweet part and leave everything else in the bowl.

To see this trick in action, imagine you're facilitating a training with staff of a residential school, many of whom have been there for a long time, and the school is thinking of changing their residential facilities from all being single-gendered to at least one all-gender hall. You're job is to help the staff understand the change, and you get this comment:

Participant: "You know, I have been here a long time, before many of you were even born, and I've seen a lot of changes, but this is one I just don't get. Our kids need to be safe, feel comfortable, be taken care of in their halls, in their homes, and I just don't think we can do that if we allow both sexes in the same residence halls, I just don't know if all this transgender business is a good idea."

You got a lot to work with here, lots of chocolate in that bowl. Let's get to picking.

Facilitator: "Yes, I couldn't agree more on how important it is for you to for our kids to be safe, feel comfortable, and be taken care of; this place is their home. And this change will help the school be safer for transgender and gender non-conforming students, who, right now, are some of the most vulnerable and at risk."

Or, another pickable piece would be the two times this participant [bravely] expressed a lack of understanding:

Facilitator: "I appreciate you sharing your concerns. I heard you say a couple times that you just don't understand this change, and I want to applaud you for essentially saying "I don't know." That's hard, and it's exactly why we're here having this conversation, so we can all figure this out together. What are some specific points you're struggling with?"

And the list goes on. YARing actually gets easier, not more difficult, when you have a really talkative participant. In a long rant, you don't have to affirm every point they make, and can instead pick out only the ones that will help the group accomplish the learning you're charged with.

PRACTICE MAKES (MORE) PERFECT

What is truly wonderful about this concept, and many concepts in this book, is that it is not just an in-facilitator-mode skill. Practice this at home! We have found it useful in all areas of life. Whenever you disagree with someone who is saying something, you can release your facilitator skills into the wild and practice your "yes, and...." When we practice in our daily lives, it makes those pressure situations all the easier to navigate when you've got a couple of good, yes-and-I-totally-disagree-with-you-and-I'm-going-to-leave-your-reality-intact-while-I-disagree moments.

It's easier to shut someone down if they misspeak. It's easier to say no. It's easy to tell someone why they were wrong for thinking something, and to curb "bad" thinking with quick corrections. But we're not here for easy. We're not here for "no." It's not easy to create a space where everyone truly feels like they can explore freely, able to be themselves and share their experiences, and know that they won't be shamed for what they're bringing to the table. But that is what facilitation is all about, about creating and holding that space for everyone to bring their voice to the table: and "yes, and..." will help you do just that.

Asking Good Questions?

"Draw a monster. Why is it a monster?"

- Janice Lee

t is through good questions that facilitation shines. And the shiniest facilitators around have the ability to identify a good question, ask it in a non-judgmental, non-shaming way, and then use the response given to further catalyze learning.

We define a good question as one that intentionally leads to learning, whether that's an expected direction or not. Good questions are productive questions. Good questions facilitate further exploration and curiosity.

Good questions don't necessarily have to be answered aloud; sometimes a question itself, without an answer, will prompt introspective learning. Good questions also don't have to follow a particular format; every type of question can lead to learning, and every type of question can stint learning. Let's start by exploring that.

UNDERSTANDING DIFFERENT TYPES OF QUESTIONS

Most people, in learning to become facilitators (or, you know, during life), are taught two types of questions: open-ended questions (that don't have a "yes" or "no" answer, which we're told are good) and closed-ended questions (yes" or "no" answer, which we're told are bad). That's a start, but a great facilitator has far more than two types of questions in their back pocket, and knows all types of questions can lead to learning, depending on how you use them. Here are a bunch of different types of questions we rely on in every facilitation:

Challenging questions: a way to suggest an alternative idea, or a different way of thinking about something, that grants agency to the person who had the idea you are challenging. *Example: "Is it possible that the alternative [to what you just said] might be true for some people? How so?"*

Clarifying questions: often a rephrasing of another's point or question, these are used to ensure that what was communicated (from the other person to you) was heard. *Example: "What did you mean when you said [...]?"*

Gauging questions: to get a sense of where someone, or

a group, is at, mentally, emotionally, or physically. The responses can be used to determine what activities or discussion is needed next. *Example: we often use "how would you define gender identity" as a gauging question, and based on the complexity of their explanation (e.g., "gender exists as a spectrum" vs. "GENDER IS PENISES OR VAGINAS!"), we know how to move forward.*

Leading questions: often used when you have an answer to in your mind (e.g., a particular learning outcome) and you use to help participants get there (mostly) on their own. *Example: "How might [...] be a factor in creating [...]?"*

Probing questions: follow-ups to a broader question, probing is pinpointing a specific part of someone's answer (or a sentiment expressed in a group) and asking questions to highlight, expose, or better understand where it's coming from. *Example: "Can you speak more to that idea? Why is it important?"*

Reflective questions: prompts for the participants to think about themselves, what they've learned, who they are, or what they are engaged in currently, with the hope of bringing that understanding to the greater group as an opportunity for learning. *Example: "Have you ever experienced [...]? What did it feel like?" (We dig more into this second question in the chapter on Learning from Emotions.)*

THREE MAIN CATEGORIES OF QUESTIONS, INTO WHICH ALL THE ABOVE TYPES MAY FALL

So you may have noticed that we didn't include open-ended vs. closed-ended questions in the list above. And you might be thinking, *"Um. Dudes. What trickery is this?"* No trickery! We don't think of these as *types* of questions, but as overarching categories, into which all of the types of questions we have above (and others) can fit.

With that said, following are three categories of questions. Read closely: there is more to closed-ended and open-ended questions than you may think!

CLOSED-ENDED QUESTIONS

A closed-ended question is any question to which the response is known by the responder, and is finite. Oftentimes, these come in the form of "yes/no" questions (e.g., "Are you enjoying this activity?"), but they can also come in other forms. Introductions are another common time when a facilitator may use a closed-ended question, like when asking participants to disclose demographic information about themselves (e.g., "What are your jobs?" "Where do you live?").

The two key elements to closed-ended questions are that the responder *knows* the response before you ask them (it's already floating around in their mind—no digging is required), and that the response is *finite* (it has an anticipatable end). With these things in mind, closed-ended questions are great for a variety of circumstances:

* When you are trying to get a lot of input from the group without using much time. *Example: "Are people good to continue for the next 15 minutes or do we need to break now?"*

* When you have a really large group, and you're trying to make what would otherwise be a teaching or lecturing session more interactive. Having participants raise their hands if they identify with a statement is a form of a closed-ended question. *Example: "Can I see a show of hands of anyone who has ever been asked to speak as a representative of their group?"*

* If you don't know the group well, and don't yet have a strong sense of what direction the facilitation should go. *Example: Would folks like to spend more time on the concept of universal design or are we ready to move on?*

OPEN-ENDED QUESTIONS

An open-ended question is any question to which the response may or may not be known by the responder, and is infinite. A common open-ended question facilitators use is "How did that activity make you feel?" A common open-ended question you may use every day is "What's new with you?"

The key thing about open-ended questions is that the response is potentially infinite[1] (it does not have an anticipatable end). With this in mind, open-ended questions are perfect complements to closed-ended questions, and they are

---

1   If you're struggling with the finite vs. infinite responses concept, consider this example: **"What is your name?"** vs. **"Why is that your name?"** In the former question, the response is limited at most to the person's full name (and perhaps a nickname, "...but my friends call me 'Lunchbox.'"). The second question is limitless: the responder might tell a story of how their name was chosen, they might talk about the origins of the name, they might do both of those things and something else, or they might even state that they're uncomfortable with the question, or refuse to answer—and what matters here isn't what the responder chooses to say (because whatever they choose will likely have a limit), it's what they were able to choose from. It's the limitless choice they have that makes this question "infinite."

also helpful in many other situations. Consider the following cases:

* When you are trying to better understand an individual participant, and have the time to give them the agency to choose exactly what and how much to disclose. *Example: After asking "Did y'all enjoy that activity?" if someone answers "Yes!" you might ask "What about it did you like?"*

* When you have a small group, and there is the ability to really get to know one another. *Example: "What are you all hoping to gain out of this experience together?"*

* If you know the group well, or have a feeling they'll know where they want the facilitation to go. *Example: "Today, we're hoping to gain a better understanding of [...]. Where do you think we should start?"*

CO-CREATIVE QUESTIONS

A co-creative question is any question to which the response is likely unknown by the responders (and may not even be known by the asker), and is infinite. Co-creative questions allow the responders to learn about a concept they may not have realized they knew about, through their own responses (and the responses of others).

A common format for a co-creative question is taking two responses someone has given and combining them into a new open-ended question (e.g., "So, earlier you said [...], and you feel [...], how/what/why/who [...]?). One of the simplest co-creative questions is "Why?" Asking a participant "Why [...]?" repeatedly, diving ever deeper into a concept—a tenet of the Socratic Method—can lead to tremendous learning. However, if they spend a lot of time with toddlers, it might also lead to traumatic sobbing. Beware.

There are two wonderful things about co-creative questions: [1] they can simultaneously highlight for a person the knowledge *they've* acquired, and turn it into learning for everyone else; and [2] they often present opportunities for you, as the facilitator, to learn from the group. You might be *leading* the participant in a direction when you ask one, but because they're open-ended, the response might be (and often is) something you've never thought of.

Here are a few scenarios where co-creative questions are ideal:

* When there is a participant (or the group at large) who just doesn't seem to be "getting" or connecting with whatever content you're talking about. *Example: "I am hearing that in your experience, men are always more into sports than women. What would it mean if there were a group of men who didn't like sports? What would that say about them?"*

* If there is pushback, or you are talking about a controversial, polarizing issue. *Example: "What is the worst case scenario you can imagine if [...]? What are things we could do to prevent that from happening?"*

* When you have a lot of time to explore without the promise of gaining any learning from that use of time (co-creative questions are always a risk, and often require several follow-up questions to work). *Example: "I am hearing different thoughts on whether parents should have paid time away from work when their children are born. Why do you think we all have different opinions on this topic?"*

Now that we know the anatomy of good questions, let's talk about how to put them into action in your trainings. *Can we call this the physiology of good questions? Why might it annoy you if we keep using more and more taxonomies to define questions? Are we still friends?*

PUTTING TYPES AND CATEGORIES OF QUESTIONS TO WORK

Remember, as we said in the beginning of this chapter, the main thing that separates a good question from a bad one is how much learning it evokes. Keep the following things in mind—in addition to all that jazz we said above—when choosing your questions, and you will be able to sit back during a facilitation as your questions do all heavy lifting.

PREP

Asking good questions is not only an improv-like "in-the-moment" skill. Taking time when you're prepping for the workshop to consider what kind of questions you should ask, how you should ask them, and what type of learning and answers you're looking for is essential to asking good questions.

One way to do this is to write up discussion questions beforehand for each activity you're facilitating, and then jot down a few bullet points of learning you hope these questions will lead to. That way, even if those things don't come up from the group, you can plop them on top yourself—little cherries on the facilitation sundae.

One way to do this is to write up discussion questions beforehand for each activity you're facilitating, and then jot down a few bullet points of learning you hope these questions will lead to. That way, even if those things don't come up from the group, you can plop them on top yourself—little cherries on the facilitation sundae.

SEQUENCING

The order in which you ask questions can be as important as the questions themselves. Imagine that in facilitation you are constructing a building with your group members. The answers they provide to your questions, and the learning that takes place, are the bricks; the questions are the scaffolding that allows you to build higher and higher. You have to start at the bottom and work your way up[2].

If you have heard of the debriefing technique known as the "What? So what? Now what?" you already know a little bit about sequencing questions. This technique empowers a group to define the learning that is taking place ("What?"), why it is important in their own lives ("So what?"), and then to consider how they might integrate the learning in their future life and work ("Now what?").

Another model we've really found helpful to keep in mind when sequencing our questions is the experiential learning model[3]. This model has 5 stages: Experience, Share, Process, Generalize, and Apply.

Experience is the actual doing of the activity or having of the discussion. You may need questions in the actual activity as well, but these aren't your processing questions.

Share is talking directly about the experience, reflecting on the experience of doing. *"What was it like to do that*

---

2 Or you could build a really high scaffolding and just start dropping bricks of knowledge on people from the sky. While it sounds like the facilitator edition of Angry Birds, we don't recommend it.

3 A handy handout on this model can be found at this link: http://bit.ly/UTMlm

activity? *Did you have any thoughts or feelings you didn't expect? How did it feel to be asked to share with a partner? How did it feel to have to step into the circle?"*

Process is the next layer in, when we are starting to get at the heart of the learning goals of the activity. *"What did you learn during the course of that activity you hadn't considered? What kind of insight did you learn about yourself during this activity? Why do you think I had you step into the circle rather than stepping out? What might that represent?"*

Generalize is when we start to bring the processing outside of the activity. We do this by asking questions that allow participants to start seeing the bigger picture importance of the learning they were just processing. *"Where else in your life do you think that type of experience may occur? In what other areas of life could the things we were just talking about be important?"*

Apply is when we get to a place where participants integrate what they are learning to specific situations, to their jobs, to their relationships, or their life. The questions you ask here will hopefully bring what is learned in the training out into the world. *"How do you think this kind of insight could be incorporated into your job or into a group you're involved with? If you had to teach someone about something you learned in this activity, how would you do it? What did you learn from this activity that will change how you interact or engage in the future?"*

EXECUTION

The *way* we ask the question matters too. As facilitators, much of *how* we do matters more than *what* we do, and this is true here as well. Here are some elements to keep in mind that can impact the outcome of your questions:

Tone. Tone is huge for creating those shame-free learning spaces. We want to answer questions when someone is genuinely curious about the answer, so it is important as facilitators that we clearly communicate with our tone our curiosity about the respondent's answer.

Answering first. As a facilitator, when you let folks know what you think first, some may internalize this as the "right" answer, and be less willing to share their thoughts. On the other hand, it may lower the risk and invite more people to share. This is a tricky balance. If you want your participants to be vulnerable, it helps if they know you're willing to be vulnerable as well (and modeling this can break the ice); but reserving your opinion until the group has responded will help prevent you from swaying their thoughts too much.

The "awkward" silence. Silence is important ingredient in facilitation. It affords time for folks to internally process the question, to build up the courage to talk, and it can be a welcome and needed pause in the flow of the workshop—a breath of fresh air. If you're asking complex questions, reflective questions, then folks are going to need time to think through them. All of this creates moments of silence in the room. That's okay! Silence feels different for different people, but it is almost always necessary for good questions to grow into great questions. If you, as the facilitator, are uncomfortable with silence, it will likely feel awkward for everyone in the room. If you embrace the silence, you're opening the door for others to do so as well.

ASKING FOR FORGIVENESS AND PERMISSION

What we've laid out above is meant to serve as a road map. Questions are (without question) the most important vehicle in which you can facilitate a group from point A to point B. And like all road maps, sometimes they can get you exactly where you need to go, and sometimes you read them wrong and they get you lost. This couldn't be more true than with asking questions.

There will be times when a question you ask takes a group from point A to being even more stubbornly at point A; or when you ask a question hoping for B and you end up lost in X, Y, and Z; or—the thing many of us dread the most—when you get a group to point B (*Yay! Go you! You're awesome!*) then ask a question that undermines what the group learned, and you all find yourselves back at A (*Shit. Shit. Shit. Shit.*).

Questions are risky. Facilitation is risky. As we discussed before, the temptation to lecture comes from wanting to have full control. With more control there is less risk.

There's this phrase that amuses Sam[4]: "It's better to ask for forgiveness later than permission now," meaning do what you want (even if you might have not gotten a "Thumbs up!"), then apologize after. By choosing to facilitate learning, instead of lecturing or teaching, we are, in a way, asking our

---

4 It's a miserable model for consent. The expression says "I know you'd say no if I asked, so I'm not going to ask, and trust that you'll be cool with this afterward." It's emblematic of facilitation, because 100% informed consent isn't possible in an uncharted journey that could end up in a place you never expected it going.

group for permission now to ask for forgiveness later. We're asking their permission to involve them in the learning every time we ask them a question; then, when things don't go exactly as we had in mind (as they never will—not *exactly*), we ask for forgiveness as we redirect. And this continues throughout the experience.

Facilitation is inviting the participants to contribute to the learning with every question we ask, while accepting responsibility for the learning (so we can build on it) and lack of learning (so we can refocus) that's already happened. It's going in knowing that we're going to fail, but hoping that we can fail forward together.

And with great risk comes great reward. The reward of asking good questions is seeing a light go on in a person's eyes, and the feeling in your gut that they get something important that comes with it. It's a brighter light than you've ever seen when you taught someone something, because through asking the perfect question, we've enabled them to teach it to themselves. It's learning we know will stick, and that they will carry with them into their life. Our goal was to get them from point A to point B, and the best questions will leave them walking eagerly on their own through B toward point C.

Safe Space for Vulnerability

"Vulnerability is our most accurate measurement of courage"

- Brené Brown

O n one side of the stage, high above the crowd, a trapeze artist chalks his hands, pats them on his legs, then grips the bar. He takes a small breath, shakes off his fear, and steps off of his platform—after a moment's fall, he swings. Swooping toward the ground, then toward the sky, he releases his grip and throws his body into a spin. Suspended in the air, for an instant he's weightless, but gravity soon takes its grip and he begins to plummet.

A few moments earlier, another artist on the other side

of the stage, having chalked her hands and cleared her mind, recentering herself, she inverts on the trapeze; and hanging from her knees high above the stage, she takes her leap. Now, she is swooping in a large precious arc toward the first artist, who is in a free fall toward the stage. She reaches out, locks arms—his life is literally in her hands — and safely swings them back to her platform.

The crowd erupts in applause. Most of the audience are rapt in awe and disbelief—unsure of how either artist was capable of what they did, or everything it took for them to succeed in their feat—but a few spectators are looking up at them, high on their platform, thinking, "I'd like to take that leap."

The first artist is the embodiment of vulnerability: throwing himself into the air, uncertain of his safety; trusting that this risk won't result in his undoing, he surrendered himself entirely into the hands of another.

The second artist is the embodiment of courageous compassion: planning to catch before the other needed it; having already made the decision to do everything she could to catch him, no matter how twisted or turned he became in his leap; and inverting herself, shouldering a different kind of risk to ensure the connection.

In this chapter, we discuss the complementary pair of traits that are vulnerability and courageous compassion, two things that combine to foster risks without regrets, leaps without deadly falls.

This complementary pair is necessary get the most out of all the concepts that follow this chapter (the *prestige* of this book), and in order to succeed in this feat, you'll need to draw on all the lessons you've learned in the chapters that came before it (our *pledge*). This is the *turn*. Pay close attention, or you might miss it.

[RE-] INTRODUCING VULNERABILITY

Vulnerable is generally thought of as being susceptible to emotional, physical, or psychological harm. Vulnerability, in this understanding of the term, is generally unavoidable (you can never absolutely protect yourself from all harm) and simultaneously something to be avoided at all costs (most people do not seek out harm). Vulnerability gets a bad rap. In the context of this book, we'd like you to meet a different connotation of the word.

In this book, the word **vulnerability means *making oneself* susceptible to emotional, physical, or psychological harm**. In this way, vulnerability is as much of an action as it is a mindset. It's a decision. It's a process. And, above all, it's something we see as desirable, healthy, and even necessary for fostering connection and powerful learning.

Our understanding and celebration of vulnerability comes from Dr. Brené Brown, whose research has informed our facilitation work as much as it has our lives in general[1]. It was through her work that we further solidified our beliefs

---

1 Seriously. Nothing lights us up as much as the opportunity to gush about Brené—her work, her attitude, her angle on life. We're going to do our best to not make this chapter into a Brené Brown Fan Blog (which we don't have...yet), so let us instead take a moment to say this: we recommend everything we've ever read or seen from Brené to every facilitator, trainer, educator, and human. At the very least, watch her TED talks, read *Daring Greatly* then *Rising Strong*, then get back to us if you're somehow not convinced. All of her work, in one way or another, informs this chapter (and, truly, this entire book [and — hell, let's be real—everything we do in life ever all the time every day oh gosh this footnote has spun out of control okay we'll stop]).

that vulnerability isn't something to be avoided, but something to be embraced, both for us as facilitators, and also for the participants in our trainings.

WHAT DOES VULNERABILITY LOOK LIKE?

The analogy that we used at the opening of this chapter demonstrates a physical display of vulnerability, and also a particularly loud one, but vulnerability takes on many forms and volumes. Sometimes it's physical, but for many of us it's more often opening oneself up to emotional or psychological pain. Sometimes vulnerability is subtle, tiny, and almost invisible. What feels vulnerable for one person may not feel vulnerable for another, and there may be no one act, decision, or mindset, that is universally vulnerable. But to paint it with a broad brush, vulnerability looks like risk.

Vulnerability is someone letting their guard down. It's opening the drawbridge to the castle when you feel there is an enemy is at the gates, and asking them kindly not to storm in. Vulnerability is someone stepping outside of their comfort zone. It's playing a game when you're not sure you can win. Vulnerability often feels like displaying weakness when you want to be displaying strength.

In facilitation settings, vulnerability takes a few common forms:

* Saying "I don't know"—as a facilitator, who feels pressured to be seen as an expert; or as a participant, who is afraid to acknowledge they have room to grow.

* Engaging in an activity, discussion, or process without a clear assurance of where it will go—as a facilitator, for whom this is new territory; or as a participant, who has to trust the facilitator to be their guide.

⋆ Sharing a perspective that is personal, meaningful, unpopular, or otherwise scary—as a facilitator, who may lose the group's trust or respect; or as a participant, who may be mocked, attacked, ignored, or worse.

WHAT DOES VULNERABILITY FEEL LIKE?

The process of vulnerability is uncomfortable. There's a phrase we use a lot in conversations about complex social issues (like oppression, or identity) that goes, "If you're comfortable, you're not engaged in the conversation." This is because to fully engage in a controversial conversation is an act of vulnerability, and the discomfort that comes with it is generally palpable. We feel it in the pits of our stomachs, in our quickening heart rates, the sweating of our palms, the anxious tapping of our feet, the clenching of our jaws and tensing of our shoulders.

Sometimes the process of vulnerability brings about a fight or flight response in our minds. We feel threatened, and in turn see options of "threaten back" or "retreat." Things move quickly—too quickly—and we don't have time to think them through. Risks get highlighted, magnified to an overwhelming scale, and are sometimes all our mind is able to identify.

And sometimes the process of vulnerability evokes an intense emotional response. From fiery anger to profound sadness, the range is wide and the experience is often one that feels decidedly irrational. Part of us knows *I shouldn't be feeling this* (e.g., "Why am I crying? All I did was tell the group how grateful I am to be here...") while another part of us knows *I should absolutely be feeling this* ("Of course I'm crying. I just told the group how grateful I am to be here!").

We're using this phrase "the process of vulnerability" because all of the above might happen at any point in a series of moments: when you're considering a vulnerable action, when you're acting vulnerably, or after you've acted.

After reading the above section, you might be remembering back to our phrase "celebration of vulnerability" and thinking, "Please don't invite me to a Meg and Sam party." Yeah, yeah, we know. Sweaty palms isn't an easy sell, and if we somehow didn't hook you with the allure of irrational sobbing, then give us one more shot.

Let's revisit what we highlighted as common forms of vulnerability that present themselves during facilitation, and see if we can get you all aboard the S. S. Expose Yourself .

Vulnerability is saying "I don't know." We don't know about you, but for us it's hard to imagine learning happening in a setting where people are unable to confess a lack of learning. Further, when we do a side-by-side comparison of "sweaty palms" and "giving inaccurate information that may damage someone's career or cause serious and irreversible harm because of winging an answer someone felt unable to not answer" we see an obvious, sweaty winner.

Vulnerability is engaging in an activity, discussion, or process without a clear assurance of where it will go. If you recall back to previous chapters, you'll remember that facilitation (compared to teaching or lecturing) requires us to let go of individual control. We might end up sobbing uncontrollably, or we might end up asking the perfect question that opens a floodgate of learning, and sometimes we'll do both of those things at the same time.

Vulnerability is sharing a perspective that is personal, meaningful, unpopular, or otherwise scary. Not to belabor the point, but, again, this almost is the goal of facilitation. None of us can be truly neutral, so anything we add to a space is going to push or pull, and we can't know how intensely others will feel that push, or how much it will pull out of us.

MEET COURAGEOUS COMPASSION

The two words are familiar. One means not being deterred by fear, danger, or pain, and the other means sympathy, empathy, or concern for the suffering of others. And like how we're using "vulnerability" in this book, our use of "courageous compassion" is based on common understandings, but with a twist.

In this book, the phrase **courageous compassion means choosing to overcome the fear, anticipated danger, or pain of *empathizing* with another's suffering.** In this way, courageous compassion, like vulnerability, is as much of an action as it is a mindset. Courageous compassion is embodied in moments, and it's carried with in us between them.

Courageous compassion is rooted in empathy, and assumes that—when we choose to—we are capable of great feats of empathy, something Sam Richards calls *radical empathy*[2]. At its most extreme, courageous compassion might be thought of as loving one's enemies, but we'd never generally

---

2 Check out Sam Richards' TED Talk "A radical experiment in empathy" for more perspective on this.

recommend you think of participants as enemies. (Though it's okay to think of some participants are enemies. You know the ones. And they know who they are. Jerks—but we love those jerks.)

What does courageous compassion look like?

In the trapeze analogy, courageous compassion was the second person who was swinging in to catch the first. While this is a helpful mental image, it's missing one piece in particular that we now think you're ready to know: what was happening in that trapeze artist's mind.

In the story, we said "having chalked her hands and cleared her mind, recentering herself, she inverts on the trapeze." What we didn't tell you was that earlier, backstage before the show, the first artist was a complete asshole to the second. And in her mind, as she was climbing the ladder to her platform, was the repeated thought of "How easy would it be for me to just *not* catch him?"

But that's not who she is. She's here to catch him, no matter how much of a jerk he is, and recentering her mind on his well-being, and inverting herself (literally turning herself upside-down for his benefit), is what's needed to ensure she has both hands free to catch him. And that, our friends, is courageous compassion. It's not just what happens (the catch, the saving of someone who is falling), it's the mental gymnastics that had to happen before the catch.

Now, what does courageous compassion look like in facilitation? In an interview we hosted with Erik Tyler[3], a facili-

---

3 If you'd like to watch the interview, it was part of our FacilitatingXYZ LIVE Series, and can be found at this link: http://bit.ly/UTMei

tator and life coach, he told us that people tend to open up to him in ways they don't open up to others. We asked him why, and the conversation turned to him sharing with us that he chooses to love someone before he meets them. Further, he said that in facilitation, "it's fun for [him] to actually have the person that's least likeable feel like someone loved them by the end of it."

That is what one form courageous compassion takes in facilitation. Here are a few more:

* Finding common ground with someone who has said something that makes you feel like you're diametrical-ly opposed, often by asking "Why?" (e.g., "Why do you believe that?" or "Why did you think that was the right thing to say?") with genuine curiosity, instead of as a thinly veiled value statement.

* Being patient with a participant, or a group, when they are being obstructive or impatient themselves.

* Exploring a concept you've explored a thousand times before with the excitement of someone who is seeing it for the first time.

WHAT DOES COURAGEOUS COMPASSION FEEL LIKE?

Courageous compassion feels like internal liberation. That's probably not what you were expecting us to say, after all the sweating and sobbing we talked about above. And we understand why you may be in doubt, and we want you to know that we often experience that same doubt. The doubt, actually, is one of the things that inhibits us from acting with courageous compassion.

But the doubt isn't courageous compassion any more

than a frozen bum is snowboarding. The doubt pops up when your courageous compassion recedes. It happens when you get out of that mindset, or before and after a moment of courageous compassion. The more time you spend in doubt, the colder your bum gets, because it means less time you're actually snowboarding. And it's not just doubt. It's fear, it's judgment, it's resentment. It's a lot of things. But none of them are what courageous compassion feels like, because you can only experience that feeling when you've overcome the others.

And when you do access courageous compassion, it feels like freedom, because you're releasing yourself from of all those internal chains. It feels like disinhibited connection. It feels like trust, access, and sometimes joy. And then, after you've made the connection with the other person—and felt the freedom from everything that was preventing you from doing so—courageous compassion feels as close as you can imagine to whatever the other person is feeling.

If the other person is feeling afraid, courageous compassion feels like fear. If the other person is feeling shame, you feel that shame. You may feel another person's rage, remorse, or rejection. And in the same way that vulnerability often leads you to experience emotions that you can't rationalize, you may find yourself, in moments of courageous compassion, questioning the emotions you're feeling ("Why am I feeling this sadness?"). This question may pull you out of the feeling, or sometimes a twist of it will be an anchor to find your way back in ("Why are *they* feeling this sadness?").

Fear, shame, rage, and remorse are all challenging feelings to feel, especially if you're feeling them alone. Through reaching out with courageous compassion, no one person is alone in feeling those things. You and the other person are sharing the burden of those taxing emotions—along with the sweaty palms and spontaneous sobs that may come with them. So while they're challenging emotions, they're made a little easier to navigate when you're navigating them together.

WHY IS COURAGEOUS COMPASSION IMPORTANT FOR FACILITATION?

If you're asking others to leap, as a facilitator it's your responsibility to catch them—no matter how twisted or turned they get in the air, or how terrible of a person they may seem to be or were backstage. It may take inverting yourself, and it will always take you deciding to be swooping toward them before they need it. The only way that you can safely make learning happen from vulnerability is if you meet it with courageous compassion. And even then there's risk. You may lose your grip, or mistime your swing, despite your every intent to catch that person. And that's where the following chapters come in: we can think of them as the safety net. The first safety net is learning to navigate triggers, and it may be the most important of them all.

Triggers

"The most common way people give up their power is by thinking they don't have any."

- Alice Walker

When you're driving your car in your neighborhood, it's easy to be relaxed, even to the point of autopilot. You cruise around corners, know when there's a railroad crossing or pothole to watch out for, where kids generally run across the street—you're always one step ahead. When you're driving in a new place, or driving a vehicle you're unfamiliar with (e.g., a friend's car, a rental), the opposite is usually true: you're on high alert, where little surprises can lead to huge overreactions.

All of this became evident to Sam when he and his friend decided to rent motorcycles (that they didn't *exactly* know how to drive) in Chiang Mai, Thailand (where they didn't *exactly* know the traffic laws, language, roads, etc.). Learning how to "go" on the motorcycles was a hurdle, then they had to quickly figure out how to do so on the left side of the road (being Americans, this served up another hurdle). After about 30 minutes without dying, lulled into a false sense of confidence, Sam turned to his friend at a stoplight and said, "We're really getting the hang of this." Then they accelerated, rounded a bend, and saw, up ahead in the distance, a massive, congested traffic circle.

Navigating traffic circles, if you're not used to them (as many of us in the U.S. aren't), are tricky in and of themselves. Navigating a traffic circle on the opposite side of the road on a vehicle you barely know how to drive in a country where you don't know the language or traffic laws — well, that's what this chapter is all about.

In this chapter, we're going to talk about triggers: what they are, how they work, and how we can best navigate our own triggers as facilitators.

And that last part is the most important—and perhaps most controversial—because we're going to tell you that it's not just in your best interest to learn how to navigate your triggers as a facilitator, but it's your responsibility. If you're hung up on that idea, let us build the ladder before we ask you to leap, but know that everything we present in this chapter is anchored in vulnerability and courageous compassion.

WHAT ARE TRIGGERS?

At the time of this writing, the term "trigger" has

achieved its zeitgeist moment in popular media. There are calls for "trigger warnings" in writing and teaching, and a sizable amount of controversy around the entire issue. In fact, in doing train-the-trainers recently, when we've brought up the term "trigger," we've noticed many educators reacting in what could only be described as a triggering response. Yes, folks are being triggered by "trigger." We've achieved the trigger singularity: the meta-trigger.

If you're familiar with the term from popular media, we ask that you take a huge step back, and consider the word without all of the context, prejudice, controversy, prescriptions, or other preconceived notions you may have attached to it.

In this book, **a trigger is a stimulus that invokes a disproportionately negative response**. And that's it. A trigger doesn't have to be as extreme as an oppressive remark (though those often are received as triggers); or something that resurfaces PTSD, or a traumatic experience (though, again, these certainly are also triggers). It can also be something as comparatively minor as an eye-roll, a sarcastic comment, or someone saying "I don't care."

Similar to how we discussed that no one experience may be universally vulnerable, no one stimulus is universally triggering. You need to *have* a trigger for someone to pull it, and we all have different triggers.

HOW TRIGGERS WORK

Dr. Kathy Obear's[1] writing on navigating triggers was,

---

1 We highly recommend that every facilitator read Dr. Obear's "Navigating Triggering Events: Critical Skills for Facilitating Difficult Dialogues" chapter, which you can find at this link: http://bit.ly/UTMnt. All of the

for us, a turning point in our understanding of the concept. It also reframed for us what our role as facilitators is when we are triggered.

Dr. Obear created a model called The Triggering Event Cycle, noting the recursive nature of how we experience triggers as facilitators—and how our poor handling of our own triggers can often retrigger someone else (or ourselves, but we'll get into that in a bit). This is a great way to think about how triggers work in the context of facilitation.

In the section above, we said someone must have a trigger in order for someone else to pull it. Dr. Obear would call this a person's "intrapersonal roots." Obear describes intrapersonal roots as being any or all of the following: "current life issues" (e.g., "fatigue, illness, crises, stressors"), "unresolved or unhealed past issues, traumas," "fear and anxiety," "needs" (e.g., "for control or approval"), and "prejudices and assumptions." Her model has seven steps, which are as follows:

Step 1: Stimulus occurs.

Step 2: The stimulus "triggers" an intrapersonal "root."

Step 3: These intrapersonal issues form a lens through which a facilitator creates a "story" about what is happening.

Step 4: The story a facilitator creates shapes the cognitive, emotional and physiological reactions s/he experi-

---

direct references we make to Obear throughout this chapter pull from that writing. Further, the traffic circle model that we propose in this chapter would not exist without her work that inspired it, and only serves to build upon the powerful ideas she introduced to us. To dive even deeper into how to navigate triggers with Dr. Obear, check out her book *Turn the Tide: Rise Above Toxic, Difficult Situations in the Workplace.*

ences.

Step 5: The intention of a facilitator's response is influenced by the story s/he creates.

Step 6: The facilitator reacts to the stimulus.

Step 7: The facilitator's reaction may be a trigger for participants and/or another facilitator.

While this experience is described above neatly in seven discrete steps, we aren't always cognizant of these steps happening, and can move through the entire triggering event cycle—from being stimulated to retriggering someone else—in an instant. It's often only through experiencing the cycle several times from the same stimulus that we are able to identify that stimulus as a trigger.

With these steps in mind, let's consider an example of a trigger a facilitator might experience, and how they would move through the cycle. Imagine a facilitator who cares passionately about the topic they're facilitating, and who asks the ever-great question "Why do you think I had you do that activity?" and a participant's response is "Because you like wasting people's time." Ouch.

1. The stimulus of "Because you like wasting people's time" occurs.

2. It hits the facilitator's intrapersonal roots of a need for approval in the content being covered, because they care so deeply.

3. The facilitator sees the statement as a personal attack on them, their profession, and everything they've done in their life.

4. This starts to make them want to fight back; they feel angry; their pulse quickens.

5. An intention of "giving that person a taste of their own medicine" is formed, and the facilitator thinks of something to say that will hurt the participant just as much.

6. The facilitator says "If you were better at your job, I wouldn't have been hired to have this conversation with you."

7. The participant (or another participant) is triggered, having their competence attacked directly; and/or the facilitator is triggered by their own reaction, realizing they've just compromised their own values and ethics. The cycle restarts.

This is a relatively minor trigger, as you'll likely note. The trigger wasn't an experience of PTSD, or even that nasty a remark. It was a snide, petty statement. And yet, it had the power to derail the learning, knock the facilitator off kilter, and in retriggering, it has the potential to escalate to a point that it derails the entire training.

So what can we, as facilitators, do to prevent this from happening? Well, we have just the thing.

THE TRIGGERING EVENT
TRAFFIC CIRCLE

In teaching facilitators to navigate their own triggers, often using Dr. Obear's model as a launching off point for the discussion, we found it difficult for folks to separate "this is a thing that often happens" from "this is how this will always happen." That is, we had a hard time helping facilitators

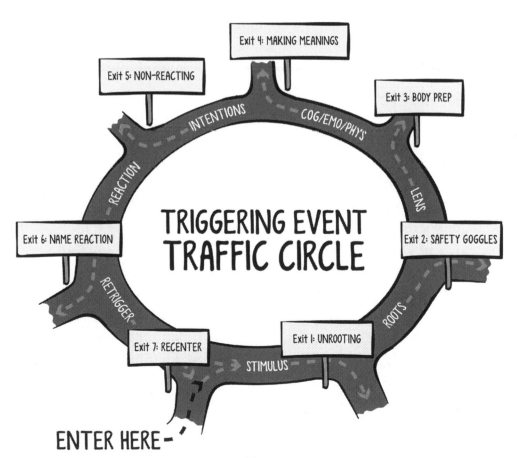

realize that while this often happens, we're not suggesting it *has* to happen. In fact, that's the opposite of what we're suggesting.

Inspired by Sam's [triggering] experience in a Chiang Mai traffic circle (also called *roundabouts* or *rotaries*), we began to use this metaphor to help folks shift their focus from the cycle itself to the exits we have available to us.

We're going to discuss this model in-depth, but first we want to highlight that the traffic circle itself — the seven segments of the road, not the exits — is the phenomenon discussed above, the seven steps of Dr. Kathy Obear's Triggering Event Cycle. Here they are presented by themselves, in case it's helpful to hold them as separate in your mind as we build on the idea.

As we said above, in our model, we are going to focus on the exits. With that in mind, know that you can only take a particular exit on the traffic circle provided that (1) you know you're on the circle to begin with and (2) you've made it far enough along to get to that exit. But if you've made it through a step of the triggering event cycle, and raised your awareness to knowing that you're on that step, you can focus on the corresponding exit.

Once on the traffic circle, you have five exits ahead of you before you do something externally that you might regret, another exit that might prevent harm in the moment, and a final exit that might keep you or others from taking another lap around the circle.

We're going to start with Exit 1: Unrooting, which is without question the most difficult exit to take. If you're feeling your hands clench on the steering wheel, know that things get easier as we go along.

EXIT 1: UNROOTING

A stimulus has occurred. You likely don't need us to tell you that stimuli are unavoidable in facilitation (unless you're doing it really, *really* poorly[2]). Similarly, stimuli that lead to triggers are also unavoidable. They're going to happen. And as soon as a stimulus that is connected to one of your triggers happens, you're cruising along the traffic circle.

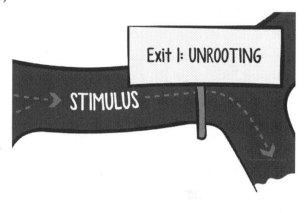

Taking your first exit, Unrooting, requires that (1) you've encountered this stimulus triggering your intrapersonal root before; (2) you've had the opportunity to engage in healing work around that intrapersonal root; and (3) through that healing work, you've managed to "unroot" this issue (i.e., disconnect it from your core sense of self in relation to stimulus, preventing it from creating the lens through which you see the stimulus).

The healing work we mention may be anything from internal, extended dialogue, to discussions with a co-facilitator, to time with a helping profession (like a therapist or counselor). This is not something that everyone has access to, the ability to engage in, or the capacity for the time and effort it takes, and as such, many of us will never be able to take the **Unrooting** exit when we're triggered, and will keep

---

2 "For this next activity, everyone is going to take a nap. And I'm going to leave."

cruising along the traffic circle to form a lens. And that's okay.

Exit 2: Safety Goggles

The stimulus triggered your intrapersonal root. Damn. This is already starting to feel bad. But you've felt this before, and as such, you've prepared yourself for just this occasion.

You reach into your mental utility belt and pull out a pair of safety goggles, and it's through these goggles that you will see the stimulus.

The goggles might be "This isn't about me. My job is to facilitate their learning." Before any training, you remind yourself what your role is, and you decide that you'll take the high road if this stimulus triggers you.

Or maybe your safety goggles are more of the "Haters gonna hate" variety, and you are able to rest in comfort knowing sometimes people are jerks.

Or, if you're like Sam, perhaps you go with the "I blame society" goggles, and you are able to process the stimulus through a lens that it wasn't intentional, it wasn't malicious, and even if it was, the person was socialized to respond in that way. It's not their fault. Similarly, Meg's go-to safety goggles are "They learned that," which helps remind her that they learned what they shared from somewhere (making it not their fault) and giving her hope for unlearning.

Whatever your brand of safety goggles might be, make

sure they're strong enough to hold up to being triggered by this particular stimulus. And, more importantly, create a pair of safety goggles that are appealing enough to you that they keep you from allowing your intrapersonal roots, having been triggered in that moment, to form the lens through which you'll see the stimulus for you — because it's rarely a safe one.

If you can put your safety goggles on, you can exit to the right. If not (and, again, that's okay!), let's start prepping our bodies.

EXIT 3: BODY PREP

Your intrapersonal roots formed the lens through which you see the stimulus. Instead of seeing best intentions, or rising above, you have a thought in your head that is less-than-positive. In the facilitator example way above, this is where the facilitator saw the stimulus as an attack on them and their profession. We've created a story now, and we are heading quickly toward reacting to that story. But we still have a few tricks up our sleeve.

As you know (both because you read it above, and because you've experienced being triggered before), the reaction generally starts internally in our body, before it manifests externally. To prevent this from making things worse, there are a few different tactics we can use to prepare our body consciously, instead of letting the subconscious take control.

Remember back to the last time you were triggered in this way. Did you close up physically? (e.g., cross legs, arms, hunch shoulders). Did your pulse or breathing quicken? Did you get angry or sad? Want to fight back or run away? Knowing what your cognitive, emotional, and physiological reactions to being triggered tend to be can help you prepare your body to get off the traffic circle.

Generally speaking, body prep is practicing adjusting your body intentionally to counteract what you end up doing unintentionally.

If you close up when triggered, body prep is practicing opening: uncrossing your legs and arms, raising your chin a bit, sitting up or back in your chair, placing your palms facing upward on the table or on your lap. If your breath or pulse start to race, body prep is slowing them down: circular breathing and other mindfulness practices can accomplish this. These are prescriptives for everyone, but they are general pieces of advice we've noticed being helpful for many facilitators.

Again, the important thing here is to think about what your body generally ends up doing when triggered, and adjusting your body in ways that intentionally offset those habits. It is you shaping the way your body reacts cognitively, emotionally, and physiologically, instead of letting the story the trigger inspired do so.

EXIT 4: MAKING MEANINGS

The story shaped your cognitive, emotional, or physiological reactions. You're noticing this in how you're thinking and feeling, and you recognize that you are on the verge of losing control. But you haven't lost control. In fact, you're approaching an exit we find to be one of the most within our control.

Consider yourself J.R.R. Tolkien, because it's time to shape some fantasy worlds. This exit is all about writing new stories (the more the merrier: meanings) to consider along-side the one your body is reacting to. Our triggered roots formed a lens through which we told our body a story—a convincing one—and if we don't come up with something else, it will be this story that forms our intentions in reacting to the stimulus.

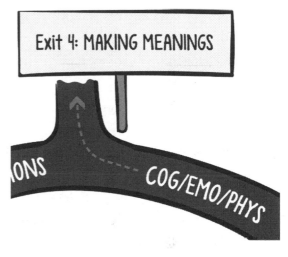

When it comes to these stories, there are three important realizations that will be helpful for you: (1) realize that you are telling yourself a story; (2) realize that this story is not reality; and (3) realize that our stories can shape our reality, or our reality can shape our stories, or we can hold them separate.

The "reality" we talk about here is the as-close-to-objective facts about the situation as you can muster. The temperature of the room, the number of people, the ways people are sitting, and the words being exchanged.

The "story" is the meaning behind all of those things. For example, a story might be *it's hot so everyone is irritated; or there are too few people in this training, so that individual person*

is feeling threatened and put on the spot; or that person is lean-
ing back because they are disengaged; or they said that because
they wanted to hurt me.

Now, with the distinction between reality and story in
your mind, you're ready to start constructing some worlds.
If in between reality (what's happening) and story (why it's
happening) you can imagine a wall: being able to separate
these concepts gives you power . If your trigger is telling one
story, and you are able to come up with a second one, that
first story loses its power. This is even more true if you can
come up with three, four, or five different stories. These can
be stories you make up in the moment, or ones you have prepared.

A great story to have in your back pocket is "I'm feeling
really triggered because I care, and I care enough not to make
someone else feel this way." All of the Safety Goggles that
you have access to can also serve as stories. From each of
these stories, or all of them combined, you can make meanings from your body's reaction, and from your time thus far
on the traffic circle, and choose the one that best aligns with
your goals as a facilitator.

The more meanings you can make, the more likely you'll
be able to exit the traffic circle here and not let the One Story
form the intentions with which you react.

Exit 5: Non-Reacting

So, you didn't make your own meanings, and instead, the
intention of your response was shaped by the story formed
by your intrapersonal roots. It's time to start thinking about
Non-Reacting, instead of Reacting. This is our last chance
to handle this internally, so it's a worthwhile exit to devote
some thought and practice to. First, let's distinguish what

we mean by non-re-acting.

Exit 5: NON-REACTING

INTENTIONS

Reacting is the effect that comes after a cause. There is no separation between the two, and the effect is determined entirely by the cause. For example, "If you push me, I'll push you back."

Non-reacting is a cause without an effect. For example, "If you push me, you pushed me. That's it. I was pushed."

Instead of a cause leading to an effect, another cause might follow a cause, something we would describe as being proactive. In a facilitation setting, this can look many different ways: (1) it can be the facilitator providing a prompt for reflection; (2) asking a question instead of providing an answer; (3) taking a moment of pause, and waiting until a participant acts; or more.

All three of the above practices are what we'd call non-reactive responses to a stimulus, and all three will help you avoid retriggering someone else, or yourself. When in doubt, the third option above is always powerful (even when not triggered), and taking several deep, silent breaths before responding (three, five, ten, etc.) is usually all it takes.

For the first two, if you're reaching for what your prompt or question might be about, the triggering event you are experiencing can sometimes provide guidance. Briefly explaining what you were experiencing, then prompting a silent reflection, or asking a reflective question, might remove you from the traffic circle. That said, this is riskier, and is something we wouldn't recommend until you've had experience navigating this particular trigger.

Finally, the most true non-reaction is no response at all. This is a time where having a co-facilitator is clutch, and they can jump in if they notice you're triggered (or you can signal them) and respond for you. Or you can ask the group to respond, "Other thoughts?" is a wonderfully generic prompt. You can take a brief break, if your schedule allows it (we are always pro-break).

Or you react. And everything that was happening internally is now visible, in one way or another, to the group. Hey—we've all been there. Let's see what we can do about that.

EXIT 6: NAME REACTION

You reacted to the stimulus. Now it's dig yourself out of a hole time[3], and we'll give you two steps to do so: name and apologize.

Saying what you are feeling or thinking is powerful. To share what is happening with you in a particular moment is an undervalued tool, both in ourselves as facilitators and for our participants.

When we say "name," what we mean is to describe—for others in the room and also for yourself—how you just reacted. In naming

---

3 Not to be confused with "a—hole time", which is when you respond to a stimulus in a harmful way and don't attempt to make things better.

a triggering response, don't focus too much on the "why," or it may sound like you're defending yourself.

Exit 7: RECENTER

Often, all it takes to defuse a triggering event is to name that it is happening. "I'm feeling triggered," might do that, and can come in handy at any point earlier in the circle, as well as now. Adding more context can also help: "I'm feeling triggered, but what was said wasn't *wrong*. It just struck a particular chord in me."

In naming how you felt and what happened, be sure you use as much "I" language as possible. For example, instead of "you triggered me," you can say "I was triggered." After naming, move swiftly into apologizing.

Your apology can be short (and it really should be). "I'm sorry for reacting that way." Or it can be a pivoting point to turn this experience into a teachable moment for others, if that fits within the goals of your facilitation. "And I'm wondering...has anyone else ever reacted in a way they weren't proud of? Can you explain what that feels like?"

Our goal here is to prevent our reaction from retriggering someone else, or from retriggering ourselves. But if we can't do that...

Exit 7: Recenter

Your reaction triggered someone else. What are you going to do about it? We have only one thing to say, in addition to the two steps we suggested above: validate.

If you notice that you've triggered someone else with your reaction (or, just in general, that someone is being triggered), (1) name what you're seeing, (2) apologize for it happening, and (3) validate their experience of it.

This all might sound like, "I'm noticing that you are feeling angry. I'm sorry that my reaction caused you to feel that way, *and* I just want you to know that it's entirely valid you're feeling angry." Or something similar. The order doesn't matter so much as the "and"-ness of it all. Make sure you don't accidentally invalidate your validation by following it up with a "but."

It's not always apparent when you've triggered someone, or when someone is feeling triggered. Different people have different triggering responses. We recommend that if you notice yourself reacting from a place of being triggered, or when there is a statement made that is likely to trigger others, you check in with the group, "How is everyone feeling after that comment?" And, if someone mentions a triggering response, do your best to help them recenter.

BE A RESPONSIBLE DRIVER

As a facilitator, you are putting yourself in a role of responsibility. It is this choice that allows us to feel comfortable stating that it is your job to navigate your own triggers, and not retrigger someone else--something we would never say about a participant in a training, or a person at large.

Learning from Emotions

"I've learned that people will forget what you said, people will forget what you did, but people will never forget how you made them feel."

- Maya Angelou

There was an auditorium full of college students, and Sam had just finished performing a show about navigating the concepts of identity and social justice. After some claps, Sam moved into an open Q&A with the crowd, where his general rule is "You can ask me anything, as long as it's not about my nipple[1]."

---

1 Sam sometimes tells a story onstage about how his mom double-dog dared him to do a big jump on his rollerblades, he fell, and ripped his nipple off. Then it grew back. So there. Now you know, and don't have to ask.

A student raised his hand. He identified himself, then explained that he often offends people by accident, by using the wrong language, though his intentions are always kind. He said "It really sucks when it happens. What am I supposed to do?" Sam could hear an intense sadness in his voice.

Sam replied, "How does it make you feel when that happens?"

"Like I'm a bad *person*."

At this point, Sam was forced to put his facilitator cap on and make a choice we often make: between the two roads of intellectualizing or emotionalizing. And like in Frost's poem, we are sorry, but you cannot travel both.

The intellectual road (where Sam might lay out steps to help the student rebound, or explain why intentions don't matter as much as the outcome, etc.) is often the one we choose. It feels safe. That path is worn, the steps are marked, the view is clear. But this chapter is about the road less traveled by, the road Sam chose that night.

WHY WE WALK THE EMOTIONAL ROAD

In our upbringing, we[2] were socialized against showing emotions in public, professional settings, or learning spaces. We were taught that emotions would get in the way of our ability to contribute or benefit. In some ways, this is true: creating a space for and acknowledging emotions does get in the way of intellectualizing, but that's not always a bad

---

2 The "we" here is meant to refer to us, the authors; however, a broader "we" encompassing "those of us in the United States," or "those of us in the West," or even "those of us socialized against emotions in public" could also work. We didn't want you, the reader, to feel lumped into a "we" against your will.

thing.

Remember the "gut feeling" difference between hearing "And" and "But" when someone doesn't agree with you? In tapping into that, we're learning from an emotion. When we talk about emotions in this chapter, we're talking about all of the responses you have to a stimulus that aren't explicitly intellectual: sometimes we hear them in our heads, sometimes we feel them in our bodies.

The benefit of taking the emotional road in facilitation is that, if it is done well, it can lead to integrated, persistent learning. We remember emotions, and emotional experiences anchor memories for us, even while we forget some of the details[3]. The experience of being personally affected by something in the moment, compared to just thinking about it hypothetically, plants deep roots, which, if nurtured, can grow into powerful learning.

The risk is that you'll get lost in the woods and not see a clear way out. This is the reason why a lot of us avoid exploring the emotional road in our facilitation, and this chapter will give you some tools that we hope will muster your courage. First, we'll discuss how to invite emotions in, then how to recognize when they're present, and finally what to do to make the most of them.

---

3 The phenomenon of better remembering an emotional experience, but losing some of the details, is discussed in the world of psych as an "affective memory trade-off." In this chapter, we're talking more about the power of localization that emotional learning has (i.e., it makes the learning important to the learner), and how that learning will be remembered. But if you're curious to read more about affective memory trade-off, here's a great starting point: http://bit.ly/UTMrpn

INVITING EMOTIONS INTO THE TRAINING

Throughout this book, we've been sprinkling breadcrumbs that will help you find your way as you venture down the emotional road.

In How to Read a Group, we discussed the various ways you can check in with participants, a skill you'll rely on in helping folks learn from emotions. In the Both/And chapter, we talked about how important it is to hold the space for your participants' varied realities. The "Yes, And..." Rule and Asking Good Questions will both be drawn on constantly as you invite emotions into the room; think of them like flashlights to illuminate your path. To invite emotions into the training, you're creating a call for vulnerability, where folks are likely to be triggered—this goes for facilitators as much as participants—and in the past couple of chapters, we discussed both of these ideas at length.

We have this chapter here, at this point in the book, because we believe emotional learning to be risky, necessary, and uniquely powerful; and doing it well demands every trick in the book.

If you're convinced that emotions are essential for learning, it's important to intentionally invite emotions into the setting. Remember, as we discussed earlier, many of us have had prior experiences with learning environments where it wasn't okay to be emotional, so we must make an effort to explicitly state that it's okay in this space.

HOW TO INVITE EMOTIONS INTO THE ROOM

We've mentioned a couple of times that it's important to actively invite emotions into your training, if you want your participants to feel comfortable accessing and sharing them. A lot of the ways you can do this well are right at the start of any group experience, when the participants are still in the process of figuring out their place in the group, the norms, and what they're going to share or not share.

You can communicate to the group that their emotions are welcome in the space, or that the training might stir up emotions. Both messages are ways of inviting emotional learning. Below are a few more specific approaches you can take.

Acknowledge that the topics we are going to be talking about today can bring up emotions for all of us and that it is okay to experience those emotions and to share those emotions in the training if relevant. Do this by stating it verbally, by including the message in any materials you pass out to the group (or deliver to the group before the training), or by asking the group "Does anyone foresee this experience bringing up emotions? Would you care to share more about why?"

Refer to other times you've done the training and let people know that getting emotional is a normal occurrence. You can tell that group that you, as the facilitator, were comfortable with people expressing and sharing their emotions, and that it's a happy occurrence when it happens. This "it happens all the time" sentiment will take the pressure off of anyone who might be the first person in this training encountering emotions, and allow them to feel like they're one of many, instead of on their own.

Name specific emotions (anger, discomfort, vulnerability, shame) that may come up for folks during the training and normalize the experiencing of those emotions. Share with participants that these emotions can often be a starting point for learning and exploration, and provide an example or two of how that might be. If the trainings you do often invoke a particular emotion, or you're hoping to stir up a particular emotion, use that as the example.

Encourage other participants to share why they think creating a space for emotions may be important. You can do this by building on the question at the end of the first point above, through an activity, through anonymous reflections, or any other way you can think of. Participants hearing from other participants that emotions are welcome, helpful, and wanted is often more meaningful than hearing it from the facilitator.

RECOGNIZING WHEN EMOTIONS ARE PRESENT

So you've invited emotions into your training. Now it's time to sit back and let the seeds you've planted take root. If you know what to look for, you'll see that emotions will bloom in many shapes and colors. While it is different for everyone, here are some common things to look for when trying to identify emotions (reflect back on Reading a Group for more pointers).

Shifts in body language often happen when someone is feeling a physiological reaction to emotions, and is trying to make their body more comfortable (consciously or unconsciously). Instead of trying to interpret what the shift means (e.g., "They close their arms, so they must be mad"), because many of us communicate emotions differently with our bodies, we're suggesting you just notice the change. If you see a distinct shift in a participant's posture, it might mean they're experiencing an emotional reaction.

Tone of voice changes when folks are speaking from a place of emotion, or trying to hide an emotional response. Many of us use a particular tone when we are speaking purely intellectually about a subject, but sound quite different when we're scared, sad, impassioned, angry, uncomfortable, shut down, or elated.

Speed of reactions change often in one of two directions when folks get emotional. If we are incited or excited, we are often so compelled to get our thoughts out there that we'll interrupt others (e.g., responding very quickly to a question before it's even finished). On the other hand, if we are shutting down or confused, we may react much more slowly to a prompt—so slowly it's viewed as a non-reaction—or mentally excuse ourselves from the engagement entirely. If you notice a participant who has been quick to respond become despondent, or a slower-to-respond participant cutting people off, there's a good chance emotions are at work.

WHAT TO DO WHEN EMOTIONS ARE PRESENT

This is the moment we've been waiting for. The emotions were invited in, we noticed them cropping up, and now it's time to make the most of them. Below we have a several-step process, and while we're presenting it numerically and ordinally, know that this can be an *a la carte* menu as much as it is *prix fixe*—each item is great on its own, the dessert can come before the appetizer, and different diets and preferences (your facilitation preferences and skills) might make some of these items more appealing than others.

1. Name. You don't have to dig into emotions in order to assure someone that it was great that they brought their emotional experience into the workshop. Sometimes we may not have time to dig into the emotions, but still want to provide a space for folks to share that part of the experience. Simply naming an emotion you notice in a participant, or asking them to name it themself, can accomplish a lot of that, and also start the learning process for other participants. Knowing that someone else is experiencing an emotional reaction to training might, in itself, be enlightening, challenging, or expand one's empathy for the material being covered. By naming the emotion, you're also giving the participant a chance to confirm or correct what you're perceiving, a helpful step before trying to build on that emotion.

Examples: "It is a really hard feeling, when we feel like a bad person." or "Bill, I noticed you clam up a little bit during that activity. What were you feeling?"

2. Validate. This is a two-parter. Here, we're encouraging that you validate both the person's emotions (i.e., it's okay you're feeling that way) and that they are sharing them with the group (i.e., it's okay that we know you're feeling that way). Sometimes, just naming the emotion will serve as validation. Letting emotions go unacknowledged can make someone feel invalidated, and can undo the trust you created at the beginning of the training that emotions were okay to bring into the space. It may feel like you didn't swing out to meet them when they jumped. The first time a participant shares something emotional, it is especially important to validate their emotion, and that it is okay that they brought that emotion into the space.

Example: "You just shared with all of us that you felt vulnerable in that moment, and I wanted to say that it can be challenging to feel vulnerable, and feel very risky to share that with others. I really appreciate you sharing that with us and taking that risk. Vulnerability is something we all feel, and I can understand why you felt vulnerable in that moment. Again, thank you sharing that."

3. Explore. Follow up your validation by asking questions to explore the emotion—the key word here is "explore," because this will be an adventure of a process. These questions can be directed at the emo person[4] themself, or at the entire group. You may invite others to share similar experiences, or ask the person to share more about their particular experience. Think of every question as being a little gust of wind that will move the sails of the

---

4 Please direct all questions to Sam in grade 7 through yesterday.

entire group toward a particular learning outcome you have in mind, and know that it's okay if you go off course.

Examples: "When have you felt that same emotion, outside of this training? And why is it important for the work we're doing?" or "Has anyone else experienced this who would like to share what it was like?"

4. Integrate. Now it's time to make some meaning. The emotion you recognized, named, validated, and explored is just waiting to be integrated into the training, the overall learning, and [with some luck] your participants' lives after the training. Integrating the emotion is taking every important element that popped up, tying them together, then attaching them to the material you're covering[5]. This is an art as much as anything else in facilitation, but here's a general formula you can use: "So, [Participant] was feeling [Emotion], and we learned [Key Learning from Exploration]; this is important to [Field/Profession/Learning Subject] because it helps you [Goal of Training]. We'll talk more about that as the training continues." What we're doing here is taking something abstract and making it concrete (i.e., answering the question "Why is it important that we acknowledged that emotion?").

Example: "So, Dr. Braff was feeling vulnerable, and we learned that a lot of you feel vulnerable frequently in your work, and you're afraid to admit this to your supervisors;

---

5 If you've seen the movie *Up*, you can think of all the elements as the balloons, the training as the house, and your integrations being the strings connecting the two. If this analogy is making you cry, that's okay. A lot of people cried during that movie, and so did we. Want to tell us a little more about why that movie made you cry?

this is important to being health care providers because being vulnerable helps you admit when you don't know something, and prevent making a mistake that might harm a patient."

ASKING GOOD EMOTIONAL QUESTIONS

When we mentioned above that learning from emotions is risky, we see the "explore" step as being where most of that risk lives. Probing into someone's emotional reaction can be downright dangerous, but there are safer ways to proceed, and to create the learning we so desire (instead of a triggering, harmful scenario we hope to help you avoid). In light of this, we want to take a moment to speak more about exploring emotions, all in the form of asking good emotional questions.

If you do have time and are ready to dig into the emotions present in the space, asking questions is a good place to start. To begin with, if you're unsure if the participant is game to share more, you can ask them a gauging question like "Is it okay if we dig into what you just shared?" If "Yes," then moving forward with good emotional questions is a go! If "No," then move along; these aren't the droids you're looking for.

Start broad. "Tell me more about that," or "Can you explain what you were experiencing in that moment?" can be a great starters to dig a little deeper into what was going on for that person. These prompts will often surface additional emotions, and uncover more paths for you to explore. As we explained earlier, you don't need to direct these to the participant experiencing the emotions: sometimes just as much can be gained from opening up the conversation to the group as a whole.

After you've heard some broad reactions, narrow your focus. "What was challenging about that feeling?" or "Why is it hard to acknowledge that emotion?" may be a great follow-up to get folks to dive in a little more. The hope here is they'll start to get a sense for why these emotions came about, why they're sharing them with the group, and what impact they may have on the training or their life.

With emotional questions, the thing to keep in mind is that these questions can often feel too personal too fast, and that for a lot of participants, talking about their emotions is not something they are comfortable with or practiced at doing.

As a rule, when asking emotional questions, as opposed to the general lessons in the Asking Good Questions chapter, constantly check in on if it's okay to move forward. Active consent, in the form of primers like "If this makes you too uncomfy that's okay, but I am wondering..." or "Nobody should feel pressured to answer this..." or "Let me know if y'all want to move on" are invaluable. It might feel like you're being redundant, and that's okay.

If you notice more emotions being stirred as you explore, which will often be the case, also be checking in with yourself mentally to determine if these are helpful to your training goals. Sometimes they are, and it's worth the time and risk to continue exploring, and sometimes you might get the feeling that the additional emotions being stirred up are leading to a landslide of emotions[6], which will get in the way of the learning and have the potential to derail the entire training.

---

6 It might sound dramatic, and, if you've ever experienced this, you'll recognize it's aptly dramatic. It would also be a great name for a pop folk album or a timeless country song.

In all of this, be ready to bail at any moment—even if you haven't accomplished what you hoped to accomplish. You often don't realize that you've crossed a line until you've crossed it, and continuing to push won't help anyone. Apologize gracefully, create a space for folks to rebound (sometimes this requires a brief break), and carry on.

TWO ROADS DIVERGED AND I–I TOOK THE ONE MORE CRIED UPON

When Sam heard that person at his show respond, the guy in the audience who said he felt like a "bad *person*," he didn't just feel the pain in those words, but he felt the pain in his own chest. Sam, too, has felt that way: that when people don't see your intentions when you make a mistake, that they're not just saying you *did something bad*, but that you *are something bad*. In choosing to make some learning from that emotion, he was also choosing to bring his own emotions into the room.

The conversation went from being about inclusive language to being about the social justice movement, identity, and society as a whole; about the difference between guilt and shame, and how we so often wield one when we should be reaching for the other. There were tears, there were deep confessions, and there was a lot of learning—for folks in the crowd, and for Sam on the stage.

It was exhausting, as these conversations often are. It was also risky, as these conversations always are. And it was worth it. The learning that came from the emotional reaction to *bad person* was likely more meaningful than anything else that happened that night—at least it was for Sam, and it's something he's carried into his work ever since.

And to us, this is what facilitation is all about. The emotions that present themselves when you're in physical proximity with other people—in ways reading a book or watching a video rarely accomplish—can catalyze powerful learning.

It's what everything in this book, used with the right flourishes, luck abound, amounts to: a moment that was, by all accounts, magical. Learning happened that the crowd—that Sam himself—couldn't have anticipated happening, as though it were influenced by some mysterious or supernatural force.

Role Modeling Continuous Learning
(or the Myth of the Expert)

"Technology's moving so fast, man. It's to the point where you can make stuff up, and people will believe you. You can be like, 'You seen the new Sony Teleporter?' People will be like, 'No, but I heard about it.' I end up saying that all the time— 'No, but I heard about it.' It means I haven't heard about it, but I like you."

- Mike Birbiglia

The great (and seemingly paradoxical) thing about facilitation is that you often become more credible as a facilitator by owning what you don't know. This isn't always the case. Some people will respect you less, or find you less credible for saying you don't know something, because there is an irrational expectation of "experts" to know everything about a particular topic.

But for many, the mark of a credible trainer is one who is willing to admit when they don't know something. And admitting that to the group, while scary, is role modeling what you're expecting of them: being a person who is willing to learn. Before we get into why it's so great to say "I don't know," let's talk about why some folks would prefer that you don't.

THE MYTH OF THE EXPERT

In most learning contexts, there's an assumed power relationship of teacher (person with power, in the form of knowledge) and student (person who receives knowledge from teacher). We discussed this earlier, and came to the conclusion in the Facilitating vs. Teaching vs. Lecturing chapter that one thing that makes facilitation so great is the redistribution of power.

In training contexts where the teacher and the students are often all professionals of some capacity, this power relationship escalates the teacher role to that of expert (a person who knows everything, and is granted authority, about a particular subject).

There are a few problems with the term "expert," defined as a person who knows everything (or close to everything) about a subject: It separates people from their journey, and imagines them only at a particular point in time; it's easy to mischaracterize someone else by describing them as an expert; and people who use the title for themselves are in danger of misleading others. Let's dig into these three issues.

Experts were all non-experts first. Folks who know a lot about something used to know as little as anyone else; this is something we are forced to forget when we think of someone as an authority. Really, an expert is someone who is devoting time to learning something and constantly practicing engaging with that topic. So maybe instead, we should think if it as "experting." And experting is a constant process; there's no standard sufficient period of time one must devote before we call them an expert, and there's no amount of time at which one stops experting, because...

Experts don't know everything. Not just everything about everything, but even within a particular functional area, nobody knows *everything*. Or, at least, it's safer to assume someone doesn't know everything than it is to assume someone does, but the term expert encourages the opposite. It encourages us to assume that a person knows it all, not to question any information they provide us, and to shame them when they don't have information to provide.

And wearing the "expert" title is generally misleading, at best. Based on the research by Kruger and Dunning (1999), the more likely someone is to say they're an expert, the less likely they are to actually be one. Termed the Dunning-Kruger effect, what they found is that as one learns more about a concept, it becomes more clear it becomes how little they actually know. While novices will rate themselves as highly competent, highly competent folks will recognize how much more they could learn. So really, the one constant thing we can count on an expert knowing, that a non-expert won't know, is how much more there is for them to learn about a particular subject.

ROLE MODELING CONTINUOUS LEARNING

As we become more comfortable with the process of *experting*, and less comfortable with the static identity of expert (and all the baggage that comes with it), there are doors that open to us that weren't present before. By walking through these doors as facilitators, we can role model to our participants something we ask of them in every discussion, activity, or engagement: to acknowledge they have room to grow, and to allow others to support that growth, while holding them accountable to it.

First, we must stop vilifying ignorance, and instead, see it as the ideal place from which to learn. Most of us are ignorant about most things in the world. We haven't had the opportunity to learn, or we were too busy, exhausted, or distracted to learn. Either way, it's okay that we don't know something, and the last thing we should be doing is making others feel ashamed for not knowing something[1].

It takes a lot of vulnerability to acknowledge our own ignorance, and often it takes a level of courageous compassion to affirm someone else's. These are things that often prevent us from being willing to celebrate ignorance as a starting place for learning.

Embrace "I don't know." If you want your participants to feel comfortable admitting ignorance, you need to be comfortable doing so yourself. And it's not just this phrase, but many other similar ones that can create a space where folks are willing to admit to something they might see as a deficiency. "I'm not sure," is another good one to start sentences with, if you're willing to give it an educated guess. And so is "It took me awhile to figure this out, but..." and other similar phrases that help highlight your own journey in experting.

---

1 Willful ignorance, which we'd describe as an intentional, obstinate, and sometimes malicious refusal to be informed, is a whole different beast. We would not recommend celebrating this type of ignorance, and we also don't see it as a healthy place from which to learn, or to engage in a conversation.

The fear response to not knowing the answer to a question is often to make something up. We do this because we don't want to lose prestige, or fall from the "expert" status we were granted or felt we had to occupy by being a trainer. Holding onto this title, especially when we feel like we're deceiving others, can be exhausting and stressful, even though sometimes we feel like it's necessary. But tricking others into thinking you're an expert by not saying "I don't know" when you don't know is not helping anything. (And neither is the fear that's forcing you to keep up the charade[2].)

Get excited about opportunities to learn. When we say "I don't know," there are a bunch of different reactions we often go through. Sometimes we feel guilty or apologetic (because we thought we should know), or even ashamed (because we're a bad person for not knowing). Once you've stopped vilifying ignorance (internally and externally), and begun embracing everything "I don't know," we hope you'll move toward a more positive reaction.

We see "I don't know" as a launching off point for genuine excitement to learn something. As facilitators who often facilitate similar types of conversations, not knowing something is wonderful: it allows you to be entirely selfish, ask questions for the sole purpose of satisfying your own curiosity, and all the while the rest of the group is also learning. Actually, they're learning two things: whatever it is you're learning, and also that it's okay to be that excited to learn.

---

2 You're only a few bad 80s songs and one dead boss away from being a real-life *Weekend at Bernie's*. Don't be a real-life *Weekend at Bernie's*. And if you haven't seen *Weekend at Bernie's*, you can watch it for an example of how exhausting and ludicrous (and comical) it is to publicly maintain a lie.

WORK IN PROGRESS

As you've read this book, regardless of your knowledge, experience, or previous interest in facilitation, we hope you've been introduced to at least one idea that was entirely new. In writing this book, we've learned dozens of things. As the book comes to a conclusion, we hope to leave you with more excitement than comfort, more questions than answers, and with more uncertainty than certainty. Our goal with a lot of this book has been just that: presenting things you thought were clear, muddying them up, then giving you a path toward re-clarifying them in a more holistic way. If we can get you to say "I'm not certain I'm ever certain," then we consider that to be a win, but there is one thing we want you to be certain of:

You can be a wonderful, powerful, inspirational person and have room to grow.

We are all works in progress. Sharing the products of our growth, knowledge, and learning is wonderful. Hopefully, the concepts in this book will help you do just that. And being open about where we still have room to grow, what we don't know, and what we haven't yet learned is also wonderful.

Allow yourself to connect with the humanity of being imperfect. It will brighten your spirits, open your eyes to the path ahead, and release you of unhelpful burdens. It will also allow you to connect with your participants with more authenticity, empathy, and sincerity. And it will always keep you in touch with your "beginner's mind," something that will keep you in the moment more than anything else discussed in this book—and can always be counted on to pull a rabbit out of a hat.

Conclusion

"It's important to remember that we all have magic inside us."

- J.K. Rowling

C oming to our mind right now are the countless times we've looked up at the clock during a training, noticed we only had a minute remaining, and thought, "Wrap up? But we've only just gotten started." Because we really have only just gotten started.

There are still a million Important Things we feel compelled to share with you, but we know we only have a minute left, so we want to leave you with just one more:

We've learned as much from writing this book as you have from reading it.

Throughout the year that this book went from a raw idea to a refined manuscript, we have been constantly challenged.

We've been challenged to hold ourselves accountable to these concepts, both in our facilitation at large and in the facilitation of co-authoring this book itself. Writing these things down makes it ever more apparent when we fail to live them out (e.g., When we accidentally shut someone down with a "but;" or don't meet their vulnerability with courageous compassion, and witness them crashing down to Earth).

We've been challenged to prioritize and reprioritize what's important—and really what's necessary—for facilitators to know in order to be effective facilitators. Because, in our guts, we know that *everything you have at your disposal is necessary for effective facilitation*. When we interview other facilitators, the list of requisite traits that come up are as diverse and numerous as there are facilitators in the world. So, who are we to say these eleven trump any of those infinite others?

We've been challenged to be okay with giving you something, even if we feel that something is incomplete—we've had to convince and re-convince ourselves that an imperfect something is better than a perfect nothing. We were constantly resisting the urge to write more—more examples, more anecdotes, more explanations—in order to write *just enough*. Enough that it pushed, but didn't overwhelm. Enough that it elucidated, but didn't convolute. Enough that after you read it, you felt like it was worth your time, but not too much that you didn't think you had the time to read it.

And in all of these challenges, we see a common thread:

we are resistant to acknowledge our imperfections, or present something that is imperfect, because we so much want to do right by you, our reader.

As facilitators, despite our best intentions, we will always end up falling short, in some way or another. We'll get in the way of our participants' learning. We'll speak too hastily, or add too much. We hurt when we're trying to heal. We generate confusion when we're trying to find clarity. And for those of us who, in stepping into the role of facilitator, place upon our shoulders a mantle of unconditional responsibility, these shortcomings can keep us from acknowledging the good we've done.

Sure, you understand that facilitation is a nuanced skill, and that like all nuanced skills there is no one right way to do it, everyone approaches it differently, and the only way to master it is through practice—hundreds of hours of practice.

And you also know the difference between facilitation, teaching, and lecturing, and know that all three have merits. No one of the three is universally better than the other two, but deciding which engagement style to use is about agency and participation.

You've seen through the fallacy of neutrality. And you can name your bias in a way that will create a more open space for everyone to learn. Knowing if you're doing this well requires that you know how to read your group—how to listen to what they're saying, in all the ways they say things to you—and what to do with that information, something you're now familiar with.

You can add to participants realities with "And," instead of demolishing them with "But." Like the masters of improv, you can use the "Yes, And..." rule to do so.

There are now dozens of different types of questions up

your sleeves, and you know that how you say the words matters as much as the words you use to do so. In no situation is this subtlety more important than in trying to create a space where people can safely learn from vulnerability. And you know that it will take courageous compassion on your behalf to hold that space.

Yeah, you can now see the exit signs to navigate triggers, and a comfort in inviting emotions into a training, and learning from those emotions.

And, finally, you know that you don't need to be perfect, but instead that you should be modeling your imperfection. It's okay to reveal areas where you still have room to grow, and in doing so you will make others more willing to do the same.

But we still feel like there's so much we have yet to cover.

So here, in conclusion, we will provide you with a final piece of comfort in the form of solidarity: we are not experts, we are not perfect, we are works in progress, and we are on this journey together.

"We do not need magic to change the world,
we carry all the power we need inside
ourselves already: we have the power to
imagine better."

- J.K. Rowling

Acknowledgements

We want to thank, first, all of the participants in our trainings who, over the years, have been unknowing guinea pigs in the creation of this book. We learn so much from our participants, and it's you who keep us motivated in this work.

We also owe more than we could name to the facilitators, educators, researchers, and writers mentioned throughout the text and footnotes of this book. As much as this book couldn't exist without the participants who allowed us to facilitate, we not have been able to continue improving our facilitation techniques without the wisdom of those thinkers and sharers.

A huge "Thank you!" to Alice for jumping in on the copy-editing process on this book when we needed you, and for coping with our singular "they."

Following, we're going to break from "we" speak and take a personal moment to thank the people who, in our individual lives, had an impact on this book.

SAM'S THANKS

Andrew was the person who taught me my first facilitation magic trick, and many more after that. He was the first person who, in any sort of a formal capacity, provided me with explanations to how facilitation worked, pointers for doing it better, and techniques to use in different situations. Maggie first taught me about co-facilitation, as my co-facilitator and buddy. Kelly taught me about facilitating amongst differing power dynamics in a group, and how to listen. The names could go on and on, but what I'd rather say, I suppose, is that I first learned how to facilitate as an orientation leader at Purdue, and lessons from that period of my life are threaded throughout this book, and everything I do today. In that light, thanks to everyone who knows what BGR means.

After that, the list quickly gets massive and disparate. I owe so much of my facilitation skill set to so many different folks, from comedians who helped me find my voice on stage; to my professors in grad school who helped me think more intentionally about others' learning, development, and growth; to my sex ed colleagues who continue to push me pedagogically.

Someone in my life who asks for so little acknowledgment, but is responsible for so much of what I manage to create (this book being no exception), is my manager Chaminda. Chum, thank you for showing me a whole different side of facilitation, for facilitating so many of my projects, and for being such a positive influence in my life.

Someone who encourages me to create, and also to find calm, is my partner Jessica. Thank you, Love, for putting up with all of my projects, and making Austin home.

And a big ol' THANKS to Meg, for co-authoring this book, holding space for the meta in all of our conversations, and being a constant source of healthy challenge and unequivocal support.

MEG'S THANKS

I have always found writing to be a challenge. From bad teenage poetry, to blog posts to book chapters... it has been a battle. As an astute teacher once said to me, "Meg, you're all forest, but there are trees." The fact that you're reading a book with my name on it truly blows me away and I am deeply humbled. For this and many other reasons, my first and foremost heartfelt thanks go out to my co-author, business buddy, and friend, Sam. Without him -- his gifts of creativity, persistence, support, and his way with words -- this book would not have happened. Sam, thanks for helping me become a better writer. Thanks for being who you are and doing what you do in all the ways that you do it. For being willing to dive into this new adventure that is co-writing head first, and co-creating this book together. Thanks for inviting me on this (and many other) journey with you.

I love facilitation. And there are so many people who

have been involved in encouraging me, supporting me, and believing in me as a facilitator and educator. Andrew, thanks for being the first to tell me to keep doing it and all that have believed in me every day since. It is a true gift to get to do what you love and love what you do. There is no shortage of people and communities that have had my back, but I do want to take a moment to highlight a few. Thank you all for helping me get to this point, arrive at many of these thoughts, and find my voice to share them.

The AEE Community - Amanda & Brit - Andrew Jillings - Arianne - Ava - Caitlin - Christina - CSPeeps - D-L Stewart - Ellen Broido - Hamilton College & Rainbow Alliance - Heather & robbie - ICWES Womyn - Intern Ted - Jane - Liane - Linh Nguyen - Lisa Magnarelli - Lula - Mom, Dad, Claire, Steve, Brian & Carolyne - Preetha - Ryn - Sakhile - SJTI facilitators - Travis Hill - Trey Boynton - Yvonne Zylan

You are all part of the community that has shaped my world and left a lasting impression on me as a human, an educator, and as a facilitator. Thank you all for the gifts and words of encouragement, belief, and wisdom you have shared with me. I truly couldn't have done it without you.

And to all the coffee shops, libraries, and friend's living rooms I sat in while writing, editing, and drafting this book -- thank you! Thanks for keeping me warm, full, and for your lack of judgment in my lack of coffee drinking. I've appreciated sharing many moments with you.

About the Authors

Sam Killermann is a comedian and social justice facilitator who got his start in university orientation & first-year programs. His primary role in life now is as Director of Creativity for *hues*, a global justice collective, in which he writes, performs, speaks, and makes things. Sam is the co-creator of *TheSafeZoneProject.com*, where his favorite way to spend time is training facilitators, and he's the author of *A Guide to Gender*, which opened as a

best-seller in gender on Amazon. Sam earned his bachelor's from Purdue and master's from Bowling Green, and enjoys riding his bicycle around sunny Austin, TX, where he counts himself lucky to live.

Meg Bolger is an social entrepreneur and facilitator passionate about the process of engaging in social justice work. She founded *Pride for All*, an organization that creates projects and services focused on sparking social justice conversations. She's the co-creator of

TheSafeZoneProject.com, where she enjoys helping folks create sustainable gender and sexuality education programs. Meg graduated from Hamilton College with a B.A. and Bowling Green State University with a M.A. She enjoys flying around the U.S. to helping schools and organizations develop facilitators, all while getting asked if she's old enough to sit in the exit row.

81178978R00086

Made in the USA
Middletown, DE
21 July 2018